New Inter

A MAGAZINE OF MARXIST P

NUMBER 8, 1991

Contents

EDITOR Mary-Alice Waters

MANAGING EDITOR Steve Clark

PRODUCTION MANAGER Michael Baumann

BUSINESS MANAGER Cindy Jaquith

CONTRIBUTING EDITORS Jack Barnes, Sigurlaug Gunnlaugsdóttir, Carl-Erik Isacsson, Russell Johnson, Nat London, Steve Penner, Ron Poulsen, Samad Sharif, Jonathan Silberman, James Mac Warren

New International is edited in collaboration with *Nouvelle Internationale*, Michel Prairie, editor, and *Nueva Internacional*, Martín Koppel, editor, and *Ny International*, Carl-Erik Isacsson, editor.

Many of the articles that appear here in English are also available in French, Spanish, and Swedish. All four publications are available from New International, 410 West St., New York, NY 10014

Cover photograph: Lee Lockwood/Black Star
Cover and design by Toni Gorton

New International is distributed internationally by Pathfinder Press:
Australia (and Asia and the Pacific):
    Pathfinder, 19 Terry St., Surry Hills, Sydney, N.S.W. 2010
    Postal address: P.O. Box K879, Haymarket, N.S.W. 1240
Canada:
    Pathfinder, 4581 rue St-Denis, Montreal, Quebec, H2J 2L4
Iceland:
    Pathfinder, Klapparstíg 26, 2d floor, 101 Reykjavík
    Postal address: P. Box 233, 121 Reykjavík
New Zealand:
    Pathfinder, La Gonda Arcade, 203 Karangahape Road, Auckland
    Postal address: P.O. Box 8730, Auckland
Sweden:
    Pathfinder, Vikingagatan 10, S-113 42, Stockholm
United Kingdom (and Europe, Africa except South Africa, and Middle East):
    Pathfinder, 47 The Cut, London, SE1 8LL
United States (and Caribbean, Latin America, and South Africa):
    Pathfinder, 410 West Street, New York, NY 10014

IN THIS ISSUE

THIS ISSUE of *New International* is devoted to a number of Ernesto Che Guevara's contributions to the leadership of the Cuban revolution, centering on the economic policies he pioneered and defended. It includes an exchange of views on the lasting importance and historical weight of these contributions to the political continuity of communism. Section one contains four articles that are part of a discussion of these questions under way both in Cuba and internationally. The second section contains two articles by Guevara from the early 1960s that have long been unavailable in English translation.

The articles by Carlos Rafael Rodríguez and Carlos Tablada first appeared in *Cuba Socialista,* a bimonthly magazine published by the Central Committee of the Communist Party of Cuba.[1]

Carlos Rafael Rodríguez is a vice president of Cuba's Council of State and a member of the Political Bureau of the Communist Party. Since the opening years of the revolution in the early 1960s, he has been part of the central leadership that charted the anti-imperialist and anticapitalist course that has marked the Cuban government for more than thirty years. Rodríguez, born in 1913, was a veteran leader of the Popular Socialist Party (Communist Party) of Cuba in 1959, when the revolution triumphed under the leadership of the July 26 Movement. He helped lead the PSP to join forces with Fidel Castro, Ernesto Che Guevara, and other leaders of the July 26 Movement (as well as of the student-based Revolutionary Directorate) in forming a united revolutionary organization of Cuba's working class

ENDNOTES FOR THIS ISSUE BEGIN ON PAGE 177.

in 1961. That unified organization took the name Communist Party of Cuba in 1965.

Since 1972 Rodríguez has been Cuba's permanent representative on the Council for Mutual Economic Assistance (CMEA). The CMEA, now virtually defunct, grouped together the Soviet Union, most of the Eastern European workers' states, as well as Cuba, Vietnam, and Mongolia.[2] Within the CMEA, Rodríguez was an outspoken champion of an important international political battle pioneered by Guevara in the early 1960s: the fight to win preferential trade and pricing policies from the more industrially developed workers' states for Mongolia, Vietnam, and Cuba, as well as for other governments in the Third World facing intensified imperialist pressures. Consistent with the facts that Guevara explained in clear and reasoned terms more than a quarter century ago, Rodríguez and other Cuban leaders have continued to insist that such preferential policies are a necessary step toward redressing the way the world market perpetuates unequal exchange.[3]

Another article by Rodríguez, "Lenin and the Colonial Question," was translated and published in *New International* no. 1.

Carlos Tablada, born in 1948, is an economist who teaches at the University of Havana and has worked in the management of Cuban state enterprises. He is the author of *Che Guevara: Economics and Politics in the Transition to Socialism* (Spanish title: *El pensamiento económico de Ernesto Che Guevara*). For his work on this book, Tablada was awarded the Ernesto Che Guevara Special Prize in the 1987 literary competition of the Havana-based cultural institution Casa de las Américas. In Fidel Castro's October 1987 speech commemorating the twentieth anniversary of Guevara's death, the Cuban president pointed to the importance of studying Tablada's work. "The author," Castro remarked, "compiled, studied, and presented in a book the essence of Che's economic ideas, retrieved from many of his speeches and writings—articles and speeches dealing with a subject so decisive in the building of socialism."[4]

Over the past three years Tablada has traveled widely, speaking on the issues discussed in his book on Guevara and their relevance to the Cuban revolution today. He has visited the Latin American countries of Argentina, Bolivia, Chile, Ecuador, Mexico, Nicaragua, Panama, Peru, and Venezuela. In the fall of

1989 he conducted a two-week speaking tour of Canada, and in April and May 1990 spoke in some thirty cities and towns across the United States. In late 1990 and early 1991, Tablada toured ten countries in Western Europe: Britain, Denmark, the Faeroe Islands, Finland, France, Greece, Iceland, Norway, Spain, and Sweden. He has spoken in Italy in 1988 and 1989. He is scheduled to visit Australia and New Zealand in 1991.

Tablada is currently working on a number of additional volumes that look in greater detail at particular aspects of Guevara's political contributions discussed in the article published here and in *Che Guevara: Economics and Politics in the Transition to Socialism.*

THE ARTICLE BY Steve Clark and Jack Barnes takes up a number of points concerning the history of the Cuban revolution and the continuity of Marxism raised in the article by Carlos Rafael Rodríguez. It is based in part on a series of seminars held during an international gathering of more than one thousand workers and socialist activists in Oberlin, Ohio, in August 1989. Participants in that leadership conference came from more than twenty countries. Communist organizations in Australia, Britain, Canada, France, Iceland, Iran, New Zealand, Sweden, and the United States, among others, participated, as well as representatives from organizations such as the African National Congress, the Puerto Rican Socialist Party, and the Maurice Bishop Patriotic Movement of Grenada.

Clark is managing editor of *New International.* He is the author of "The Second Assassination of Maurice Bishop" in *New International* no. 6, and is the director of a project by Pathfinder Press to publish the Selected Works of Malcolm X.

Barnes is national secretary of the Socialist Workers Party in the United States. He is the author of several articles published in previous issues of *New International,* as well as the book *The Changing Face of U.S. Politics: The Proletarian Party and the Trade Unions.*[5] Barnes first began following the economic and political questions posed by Guevara, Rodríguez, and others in the leadership of the Cuban revolution some thirty years ago. In the summer of 1960 Barnes visited Cuba on a college research grant to study the economic transformation of Cuba under the new workers' and farmers' government. During the months he was there, virtually all the imperialist-owned industry on the island and many large enterprises that were Cuban owned were expropriated by the revolutionary government in a wave of massive workers' mobilizations. Before the end of the year Cuba had established the economic foundations that made it possible to begin the transition to socialism and necessitated centralized planning. The political and economic alternatives discussed in this issue of *New International*—elements of which were already being intensely discussed by a vanguard in 1959 and 1960— then began to be tested in practice and debated more widely and thoroughly.

The article that opens the first section is by Mary-Alice Waters, editor of *New International*. It is based on a presentation made in November 1989 at a panel on "Che Guevara's Thought in Contemporary Cuba" during a conference on "Thirty Years of the Cuban Revolution: An Assessment," held in Halifax, Nova Scotia. Waters is also editor of *In Defense of Socialism,* a selection of speeches by Fidel Castro on the thirtieth anniversary of the Cuban revolution, as well as *U.S. Hands Off the Mideast! Cuba Speaks Out at the United Nations* by Fidel Castro and Ricardo Alarcón, which documents Cuba's uncompromising opposition to the 1990-91 imperialist war against Iraq, an assault backed by all five permanent members of the United Nations Security Council.[6]

In June 1988 Waters was one of two U.S. delegates invited to make presentations to the International Scientific Seminar sponsored by the National Commission to Pay Homage to Ernesto Che Guevara held in Buenos Aires, Argentina. The seminar drew several hundred participants from virtually every country in the Americas.

The international conference in Halifax, sponsored by the Canadian Association of Latin American and Caribbean Studies, was attended by six hundred people, making it the largest gathering of its kind outside Cuba in the thirty-year history of the revolution. A delegation of forty participants from Cuba was headed by Ricardo Alarcón, Cuba's first deputy foreign minister, who is currently serving as ambassador to the United Nations. Carlos Tablada was among the Cuban delegates and spoke on the panel on Guevara together with Waters and several other participants. A reception celebrating publication of the English-language edition of Tablada's book was attended by some two hundred conference participants.

The article by Waters places Guevara's contributions, and the current debate about them, in the context of the Cuban revolution today and the social dynamics of the political reorientation of the revolution launched in 1986 by the leadership of the Communist Party of Cuba. The rectification process, as it is called, was initiated in response to growing evidence of the political demobilization and demoralization of working people in Cuba. This disorientation was a result of the political course that had begun to be implemented in the early 1970s based on economic and political policies largely copied from the Soviet Union and Eastern European countries.[7]

Since the beginning of 1990, Cuba has suffered increasingly onerous economic shortages and dislocations as a result of the sharp and sudden deterioration in the scope and terms of trade with the Eastern European countries and the Soviet Union. These countries have been Cuba's largest trading partners since the early 1960s. This new trade squeeze compounds the ongoing effects of Washington's brutal, thirty-year-long economic embargo of Cuba and its unrelenting policy of seeking by every means possible to erode popular support in Cuba and around the world for the revolutionary internationalist course of the Cuban government.

In January 1991, for the first time in three decades, the Soviet Union required Cuba to conduct much of the trade between the two countries in hard currency at world market prices. While terms to help buffer this change have been negotiated for 1991, these cushions are being phased out. There have also been increasing shortfalls and delays in deliveries of oil, wheat, and other items imported from the Soviet Union.

As A RESULT, Cuba faces substantial energy shortages, deficiencies in construction materials, and severe pressure on its limited foreign currency reserves. In August 1990 the Cuban government began instituting austerity policies to meet the economic challenges of what it calls the "special period during peace-time." In order to conserve energy and other raw materials, the length of the standard workweek has been cut by dropping the long-standing practice of working alternate Saturdays. Rationing has been extended to a much broader range of consumer items to ensure a more equitable distribution of reduced available quantities, and the production and distribution of consumer durables (refrigerators, washing machines, other appliances) and a range of light consumer goods have been severely cut back. Private energy use and purchase of gasoline and other petroleum products have been curtailed.

The Cuban government has also instituted a sharp reduction in planned new construction of social projects such as schools, clinics, day-care centers, and urban housing, although projects already under way are being completed. In addition, a number of major industrial, transportation, and communications projects have either been shut down or their completion postponed. Resources and labor have been redirected toward projects most essential to (1) advancing toward self-sufficiency in food production and (2) attempting to increase needed hard currency earnings to meet steeply rising costs of vital energy and industrial imports.

These austerity measures are having an impact on important aspects of the rectification process discussed by Waters, especially the volunteer minibrigades and construction contingents, and the application of these methods of organizing work to other sectors of industrial production itself. The brigades, based on the renewed mobilization of volunteer labor along lines advocated by Guevara, have been central to the advance of rectification during its opening few years, as Waters points out. Since 1987 the minibrigades have organized the building of much-needed housing, schools, day-care centers, and other social projects in Cuba. The construction contingents have taken on larger projects to improve Cuba's infrastructure of transportation and communications as well as its industrial capacity.

Under the conditions of the "special period," many of the new social projects that would have been undertaken by minibrigades have now been suspended in face of shortages of energy and building materials. In Havana and Havana City provinces, volunteer labor has been redirected toward agricultural work and the construction of housing and social facilities in rural areas as part of the push toward an expanded agricultural work force and more rapid progress toward food self-sufficiency.

The balance of priorities for the construction contingents has also been shifted toward projects in line with the government's current development plans, such as dams, irrigation projects, and other waterworks related to the food program; major construction projects more directly linked to plans to expand export earnings; and tourism aimed at earning hard currency.

Given the effects of these tightening economic conditions and social pressures, the issues discussed in the articles that follow are all the more central to the challenges confronting Cuba and its leadership today, including prospects for further advances along the revolutionary course of the rectification process.

THE SECOND SECTION of this issue of *New International* contains two articles by Guevara written in 1963-64. Both were contributions to a public discussion in several Cuban journals on economic planning and management in Cuba. At issue were the political and social perspectives served by alternative courses being implemented by and discussed within the leadership, and the consequences for communists in advancing the transition to socialism.[8]

At the time of this debate, Guevara was the director of the Ministry of Industry, which organized enterprises accountable to it along the lines of what was called the "budgetary finance system." An alternative "economic accounting system" was in use in enterprises organized by the National Institute of Agrarian Reform, headed by Carlos Rafael Rodríguez from 1962 to 1965. The economic accounting system was also implemented in enterprises responsible to the Ministry of Foreign Trade, directed by Alberto Mora. (An explanation of these two methods of economic planning and management and contrasting viewpoints on them run throughout the articles in this issue.)

Guevara's two most comprehensive contributions to this debate are "Planning and Consciousness in the Transition to Socialism ('On the Budgetary Finance System')" and "Socialism and Man in Cuba." Both articles—together with many others related to the matters discussed in this issue—are available in English translation in *Che Guevara and the Cuban Revolution: Writings and Speeches of Ernesto Che Guevara.*

The two polemics by Guevara published here are not contained in that Pathfinder collection. They are reprinted for the first time in nearly twenty years. New English translations have been made by *New International* for this occasion. "On the Concept of Value: A Reply to Alberto Mora," originally appeared in Cuba in the October 1963 issue of *Nuestra Industria, Revista Económica* (Our industry, a journal of economics), published by the Ministry of Industry.

"The Meaning of Socialist Planning: A Reply to Charles Bettelheim," was published in the June 1964 issue of *Cuba Socialista.* Bettelheim is a French economist who at the time was serving as an adviser to the Cuban government; his article, "On Socialist Planning and the Level of Development of the Productive Forces," had been published in the April 1964 issue of *Cuba Socialista.*[9]

These two articles by Guevara, as well as the articles by Carlos Rafael Rodríguez and Carlos Tablada, have been translated into English by Michael Baumann and Michael Taber for publication in *New International.* Except where otherwise indicated, the notes to the articles in this issue have been prepared by *New International.*

April 8, 1991

Basic works of
CHE GUEVARA

Episodes of the Cuban Revolutionary War, 1956–58
Ernesto Che Guevara

Firsthand account of the military campaigns and political events that culminated in the January 1959 popular insurrection that overthrew the U.S.-backed dictatorship in Cuba. $23.95

The Bolivian Diary of Ernesto Che Guevara

Guevara's account of the 1966–67 guerrilla struggle in Bolivia. Includes excerpts from the diaries and accounts of other combatants, including—for the first time in English—*My Campaign with Che* by Bolivian leader Inti Peredo. $21.95

Che Guevara: Economics and Politics in the Transition to Socialism
by Carlos Tablada

Quoting extensively from Guevara's writings and speeches on building socialism, explains the interrelationship of the market, economic planning, material incentives, and voluntary work. $17.95

Socialism and Man in Cuba

Guevara's best-known presentation of the political tasks and challenges in leading the transition from capitalism to socialism. $3.50

Che Guevara Speaks

Writings and speeches of a communist leader. $14.95

Malcolm X
Talks to Young People
Speeches in the United States,
Britain, and Africa

> ' I'm not an American.
> I come to this meeting as one of
> the victims of Americanism, one of the
> victims of a very hypocritical system
> that is going all over this earth today
> representing itself as being qualified
> to tell other people how to run
> their country when they can't
> get the dirty things that are
> going on in their own country
> straightened out.'
>
> *Malcolm X*
> *May 1964*

In discussions with young people on three continents, Malcolm X denounces U.S.-organized wars in Africa, Asia, and Latin America and outlines a course of struggle. 110 pp., $10.95

CHE GUEVARA, CUBA, AND THE ROAD TO SOCIALISM

Volunteer construction minibrigade in Havana. Since 1986 tens of thousands across Cuba have participated in similar brigades to build child-care centers, schools, apartment complexes, and family doctors' office-homes. Through volunteer labor, Guevara wrote, man "starts to see himself reflected in his work and to understand his full stature as a human being."

CHE'S PROLETARIAN LEGACY AND
CUBA'S RECTIFICATION PROCESS

by Mary-Alice Waters

THE POLITICAL perspectives Ernesto Che Guevara fought for as part of the leadership of the Cuban revolution—and began to implement in the Rebel Army and, after January 1959, in the ministries and departments of the revolutionary government he headed—have both political and scientific importance.

Che was one of the relatively few great Marxists of the twentieth century. He was a communist of depth and consistency who made the disciplined study and consistent application of political economy the foundation of socialist politics. He was a materialist who understood that the only way to create a society in which human solidarity reigns rather than dog-eat-dog competition is for human beings—who are products of a world still dominated by capitalist relations of production and exchange—to fight to build socialism. The new man and the new woman Guevara talked of will emerge from the collective effort to eradicate the domination of capital and of capital's companion: the debilitating and mystifying hold of the law of value on social consciousness.

Abstracted from the dynamics of the Cuban revolution itself, however, the communist policies Che fought for are rendered lifeless. His arguments become fine words on a piece of paper rather than what they were: the generalization of the line of march of a class making history and remaking itself in the process.

The biggest fraud perpetrated against Che's legacy in the

This article is based on a presentation made in November 1989 at a panel on "Che Guevara's Thought in Contemporary Cuba" during a conference on "Thirty Years of the Cuban Revolution: An Assessment," held in Halifax, Canada. Mary-Alice Waters is editor of New International.

twenty-two years since he was murdered while leading an internationalist mission in the mountains of Bolivia has been the attempt to separate him from the Cuban revolution. It was the Cuban revolution that made Che Guevara the human being he became. It was this revolution to which his leadership efforts were directed and which became his life's greatest work and accomplishment.

Over time both friend and foe, some out of ignorance and some out of fear of the communist continuity he enriched, have conspired to present Che as if he were really an outsider to the revolution he helped lead. They portray him as a brilliant and dedicated individual, but one who was increasingly out of step with the revolution's necessary line of march, its advance.

While spared the indignity of having his body stuffed and placed on display in a glass case, Guevara has nevertheless been transfigured over time. From a human being who lived and fought in the real world at a given historical moment, he became to many an icon on a wall, or an image on a T-shirt. He was reduced to a moral example alone, stripped of his other political qualities and strengths.

This idealized Che is heroic, courageous, and morally incorruptible but still a less-than-practical dreamer. He is a utopian who failed to understand that human beings are by nature base and greedy. This romanticized Che is a lonely and isolated fighter, the grotesque bourgeois image of a hero. By thus transforming Che into Saint Che, he is rendered harmless. He becomes a figure who appeals to, rather than frightens, individuals whose consciousness has been forged by the bourgeois values Guevara gave his immensely productive life to eradicate.

TODAY IN CUBA, however, a political battle is under way that can restore the real Che, rescue him from sainthood, and give life to the communist program he fought for. It is unfolding under the banner of what is called the rectification process. The working men and women of Cuba are striving to assert their power and are reasserting the truth that history is not made by divine acts, nor by unguided mechanisms. It is made by the deeds of millions.

The revolutionary potential of the rectification being fought for in Cuba stands in contrast to the deepening economic and social crises exploding in the Soviet Union and Eastern European countries, where the bitter consequences of the political-economic policies Che rejected are being played out. These events of world-historic importance are giving us all a new appreciation of Che's communist legacy. It is deeper and richer than we understood even two years ago, much less twenty years ago.

Working class strengthened

Real social forces are clashing in Cuba as the rectification process deepens. The arrest and trial a few months ago of José Abrantes Fernández, Cuba's minister of the interior and a member of the Central Committee of the Communist Party, stands as evidence of the sharp conflict. Abrantes was convicted on charges of abuse of authority, negligence in carrying out his duties, and improper use of government funds and resources. He was sentenced in August 1989 to twenty years in prison.[1]

Abrantes's conviction was even more important than the court-martial and execution two months earlier of Arnaldo Ochoa, also a member of the Central Committee of the Communist Party. Ochoa was court-martialed on charges of drug trafficking and treason and sentenced to death along with Antonio de la Guardia and two other high-ranking officers of the Revolutionary Armed Forces and the Ministry of the Interior.[2]

The events of the summer of 1989—which also included the arrest, conviction, and twenty-year prison sentence given another top government official, Diocles Torralbas, minister of transportation[3]—were not a setback to the revolution. To the contrary, they were the product of recent victories at home and abroad. They registered the fact that Cuba's working people were able to take on long-existing problems previously not confronted.

The historic victory over South African aggression in 1988 at the battle of Cuito Cuanavale in southern Angola—in which thousands of young Cuban men and women fought heroi-

ENDNOTES FOR THIS ARTICLE BEGIN ON PAGE 180.

cally—created the objective conditions to expose and confront Ochoa, de la Guardia, and their circles in a manner that led not to demoralization but to an advance in the fighting capacities of Cuba's Revolutionary Armed Forces and working people. In the aftermath of the Ochoa affair, it is clearer than ever why the future of the Cuban revolution, as well as the future of Africa, was at stake at Cuito Cuanavale.[4]

T HROUGH THE minibrigades and construction contingents that have spearheaded the rectification process, tens of thousands of volunteers have been mobilized and become part of the working class.[5] These self-confident vanguard forces have affected social relations in Cuba. Corruption, privilege, and abuse of power by a layer of the police and internal security forces—who were running the biggest international capitalist business operation in all Cuba—could be confronted as never before. Those responsible at the top were held accountable.

Loss of revolutionary integrity among a layer of individuals holding positions of authority and responsibility in the party, state, and government apparatus was not something newly discovered by the Cuban people in the summer of 1989. As Raúl Castro, head of Cuba's armed forces, noted in the course of the Ochoa affair, the people from their daily life and work knew more about the extent of the corruption than the top party leadership, and knew it sooner.[6]

Other instances of corruption and abuse had been dealt with already during the rectification process. In 1987 for example, Luis Orlando Domínguez—head of the Civil Aeronautics Institute, a former leader of the Union of Communist Youth, and recent member of Castro's special secretariat—was convicted on charges of gross corruption and sentenced to twenty years in prison.

The *Granma* editorial in September 1989 that drew the lessons of the Abrantes case emphasized that "the entire nation realized that the problems faced by the country this summer go far beyond the fate of a handful of corrupt and disloyal individuals. . . . What has happened reflects a series of shortcomings that affect, in one way or another, all the institutions of the revolution."[7] *All* the institutions.

'Two different worlds'

What was new, following three years of battles to advance rectification, was the consciousness and confidence of Cuba's working people. They were more ready than before to confront high-level corruption and abuse, to defend and deepen the communist trajectory of the revolution. The world of Cuba's working people—to paraphrase Castro, the world of the men and women who work ten, twelve, fourteen hours a day to produce what Cuba needs—had slammed into the world of a privileged and narrow layer within the army and state apparatus, and those they protected and provisioned. The confrontation between those two worlds came into the open.

"What do the lives of these gentlemen have to do with the life of a worker? What do the customs of these gentlemen have in common with the customs of our working class?" Fidel asked at the July 9, 1989, Council of State meeting. "They are two different worlds. And we cannot rest until there is one single world here: not the world of the bourgeoisie or the petty bourgeoisie, but the world of our workers, our working class, our proletariat, our farmers."[8]

A battle between these two worlds was joined on a new level in the summer of 1989 in Cuba, and the working class emerged stronger, more confident.

The war, however, has yet to be won.

What does this have to do with Che's legacy?

The generals and their friends who were tried and convicted were not accused of counterrevolutionary activity, of treason in the sense of deliberately losing a war, of passing intelligence to Washington or Pretoria, of preparing to defect to the enemy, of conspiring to assassinate fellow members of the armed forces or revolutionary government. Their crimes, *Granma* noted, were not "the work of enemy agents but rather of people coming from our own ranks. . . . They show us how, without going over to the enemy, men who have been in our ranks can inflict worse damage than any counterrevolutionary."[9]

Their crimes undermined the integrity of the revolution and its trustworthiness in the eyes of the world's toilers. The corruption they spread sapped the self-respect of Cuba's working peo-

ple. The social attitudes and behavior of these figures were alien
to the workers' and farmers' revolution, which seeks to instill in
its leadership, its army, and its police and security forces the
social values of a different class, the working class.

The July 9 meeting of the Council of State that discussed and
rejected commuting the death sentences against Ochoa and the
three others was broadcast over nationwide television in Cuba.
Several council members whose remarks were widely echoed by
Cuban working people drew directly on Che's legacy to explain
the character of the political challenge the revolution faced.

"I felt as never before how the teachings of Che have to be
relearned every day," declared communist youth leader Ro-
berto Robaina. Che taught us, Robaina said, "that the leader
must have and go without what the common people have and
go without.[10] And this is true not only of our leaders; it should
also be true of our party and our state. I'm not advocating an
absolute and facile equalitarianism that leads nowhere. I simply
believe that much harm is done by inequality when it is unnec-
essary and, above all, offensive."[11]

Lidia Tablada, director of the National Center of Veterinary
Medicine, noted that the problem confronting the revolution
could not be reduced to the corruption of a handful of individuals. She quoted Che at length, including the following passage:
"A counterrevolutionary is someone who fights against the revolution. But a counterrevolutionary is also someone who
through his influence obtains a house, and then two cars, and
then who cheats the ration system, and ends up with everything
the people don't have, and flaunts it—or doesn't flaunt it, but
has it just the same."[12]

Dealing decisively with corruption at the highest levels of
government and responding to the blows dealt the integrity of
the officers of the Revolutionary Armed Forces was not a diversion from the course of rectification but an advance along the
line of march already set.

Heart of rectification
At the heart of the rectification process, volunteer labor as a
social movement has been reborn—like a phoenix. During the
early years of the revolution voluntary work was "the brainchild
of Che and one of the best things he left us," Castro noted on

the twentieth anniversary of Che's death.[13]

Basing himself on some of Marx's most profound insights, Che explained over and over why it is that "man-as-a-commodity ceases to exist" only through volunteer labor. It is through voluntary work that social, collective labor becomes a school for communist consciousness and socialist administration, that work begins to change its character. Through volunteer labor man "starts to see himself reflected in his work and to understand his full stature as a human being through the object created, through the work accomplished."[14]

This materialist understanding of the place of volunteer labor in the construction of socialism and communism has once again come to the fore in the Cuban revolution, after more than a decade during which it withered in the face of a diametrically counterposed political perspective.

"Voluntary work," Che explained, is "based on the Marxist appreciation that man truly reaches his full human condition when he produces without being compelled by physical necessity to sell himself as a commodity."[15]

As VOLUNTARY WORK becomes an increasingly weighty component of the organization of the labor of society as a whole, producing a growing portion of the product of this labor, the scope of the domination of the law of value—and of the modern fetish, the commodity fetish, that turns us all into objects—is progressively reduced.

The movement that began with the relaunching of the minibrigades in the city of Havana a little more than three years ago rapidly took on mass dimensions. Tens of thousands of men and women threw themselves full-time into the challenge of building hundreds of child-care centers, apartment complexes, family doctors' office-homes, polyclinics, schools, bakeries, sports facilities, and more. The minibrigades have now been augmented by the expanding organization of volunteer construction contingents, a form of volunteer labor whose impact on the future of the Cuban revolution is potentially even more far-reaching.

In the last two years more than sixty labor contingents, averaging 500 workers in each, have been established. They are concentrated in the construction industry. The largest and oldest of the contingents, the Blas Roca Contingent, now has some 2,600 workers organized in twenty-three brigades, building bridges, roads, airports, dams, hospitals, hotels, and similar major projects.[16]

The numerous brigades of these contingents have been organized in the same way the columns of the Rebel Army in Cuba's Sierra Maestra mountains were formed in 1957-58, when a few seasoned cadres of the first column divided off and organized a second column, and then a third and fourth column were created out of the first two. Each new column starts not from scratch but with the high level of norms and discipline already conquered by its founding cadres.

Participation in the contingents is voluntary, subject to being accepted. A flexible workday of ten hours or more depends on the work to be completed. There is a single wage scale with no overtime pay or bonuses. Room and board is provided. Work discipline is not imposed by a separate layer of management personnel but is organized and maintained by the contingent members themselves. Equipment is cared for and kept running by the workers who use it. Administrative tasks are more and more taken on by the workers themselves, instead of being delegated to a distinct group of specialists increasingly distant from the work itself.

The volunteer labor contingents, which have transformed the construction industry, are now being introduced in a few other industries in a measured way, in particular in the production of building materials. They are starting to have a broader impact on the organization of labor. Their example is providing new experience and insight touching on the central question in the transition from capitalism to socialism: How should the working class organize social labor in order both to build a new economic foundation and in the process to transform itself and its social consciousness?

This was the question above all else that concerned Che.

If the minibrigades continue to spread and expand their role, this will advance the entire rectification process, which is above all a political process, a restructuring of social priorities to meet the needs of workers and farmers, not professional layers. Important as the minibrigades are, however, they are peripheral to the main organization of labor in basic industry, agriculture, and transport. The minibrigades set an example. They mobilize tens of thousands of volunteers from every layer of society to take on much-needed special projects. They cut across petty-bourgeois attitudes toward the working class and physical labor, and act as a giant school for learning to think socially. But the minibrigades can ultimately play only an auxiliary role that spurs economic development and the growth of class consciousness and confidence.

I F THE MINIBRIGADE MOVEMENT remains simply an adjunct to a system in which bureaucratic command planning dominates the organization of labor, then the inevitable result will be continued and increasing stratification, inequality, generalized corruption, the deadening of class consciousness, and the blocking of workers' control of production. Under such conditions, volunteer labor on the scale of the minibrigades will not be a means by which the working class can school itself in economic management and transform itself in the process of transforming the economic foundations of society. Instead, volunteer labor over time would be corrupted and turned into its opposite. It would become another administrative means to try to fulfill the bureaucratically conceived plan through work that is, in fact, neither voluntary nor productive.

This is what happened in the Soviet Union in the 1930s, when the so-called Stakhanovite movement and its accompanying "volunteer" workdays became a thinly disguised program to increase the length of the compulsory workweek and the intensity of labor.[17]

Cuba has already experienced elements of this. The volunteer brigades of the 1960s and early 1970s were transformed into their bureaucratic negation and then largely eliminated with the argument that volunteer labor supposedly contradicts Marxist—in reality Stalinist—concepts of planning. Having experienced this kind of "volunteer labor," many Cuban workers remain to be convinced that the minibrigades and construction contingents represent a qualitatively different political course and class perspective, the one advanced by Che.

Moreover, even among those who support the minibrigade movement in Cuba today, many express a degree of ambivalence about its future. They sense that the minibrigades alone cannot fundamentally alter the overall organization of labor and transform social consciousness. Other, more weighty changes must be made.

Thus the advance from minibrigades alone to construction contingents and minibrigades broadens the battle to reorganize labor on a new foundation. The heavy battalions of labor in the factories, mills, and fields are beginning to be touched on this level for the first time since the rectification process began.

The trade unions too will have to be transformed if rectification is to advance. This is not a matter of changes in leadership personnel alone, but of political reorientation. They must become organizations that are expanding workers' control and making new strides toward workers' management—organizations of a revolutionary working class that is transforming itself as it leads the building of a new society.

Nonproductive administrators and 'witch doctors'

The advance of rectification poses a challenge to the middle-class pretensions and prerogatives of the grossly inflated ranks of nonproductive administrative and "professional" personnel. The introduction of the Economic Management and Planning System in the mid-1970s, largely copied from the Soviet Union, brought with it nearly a tripling of the number of administrators and officials, from 90,000 in 1973 to 240,000 by 1984. As Fidel Castro noted in a speech celebrating the second anniversary of the founding of the Blas Roca Contingent, there were some "enterprises with more people in the infrastructure than in direct work."[18]

With the inauguration of the contingents a revolutionary challenge has been taken up: to diminish the bloated ranks of nonproductive specialists; to increase the social and economic weight of the working class. At the beginning of August 1989, of the 28,000 workers incorporated in some sixty volunteer construction contingents, only 6.4 percent were carrying out primarily administrative responsibilities.

In 1988, while 55,000 new workers were incorporated into the work force, for the first time administrative personnel and other officials were simultaneously reduced by nearly 23,000.

This reorganization of the division of labor goes to the heart of another question that Che understood to be central to the transition to socialism: the withering away of a specialized, and inevitably to some degree bureaucratized, stratum of administrators and officials. The working class itself—if better educated politically and technically, better equipped technologically, and increasingly confident of exercising control over the administration of the economy and state apparatus—progressively incorporates more and more elements of the necessary administrative tasks into its division of labor.

The anti-working-class technocrats and administrators with all their pretensions to social superiority and functional irreplaceability—"witch doctors," Castro has called them—are threatened by the revolutionary concepts of Marx and Che that are being applied by the contingents as they set an example for the reorganization of labor in Cuba. The kind of division of labor that allows a layer that administers to derive a higher social status could begin to fade away—and with it, the privileges and petty-bourgeois self-esteem they have come to consider their due.[19]

RECTIFICATION IS an attempt to chart a revolutionary course correcting previous errors made and responding to problems confronting Cuban society today. It is a line of march that would have been impossible if the Cuban people had not responded as internationalists to Angola's request for aid in defeating the South African invasion between 1975 and 1988. It would have been difficult to sustain if the Cuban-Angolan-Namibian forces had met defeat, not victory, at Cuito Cuanavale. The Ochoas and de la Guardias would have gained momentum, not lost ground, had that been the outcome.

Likewise, rectification would have been impossible without the revolutionary upsurge in Central America and the Caribbean that brought the two great victories of 1979 in Grenada and Nicaragua. Those struggles broke through the twenty-year dry spell in the Americas during which no revolutionary victory resulted in the establishment of a workers' and farmers' government. Nicaragua, Grenada, and the struggle of the Salvadoran people gave impetus to revolutionary forces within Cuba.

The rectification course set by the leadership of the Cuban revolution must also be seen in relation to the profound crisis now shaking the bureaucratic castes and shattering ruling parties in Eastern Europe and the USSR. The roots of this crisis are to be found in the system of organization of labor that has been imposed for decades on the working classes of those countries by a petty-bourgeois caste akin to the witch doctors Castro denounces. It is a system that relies on bureaucratic planning and individual and material incentives, not increasing workers' control, workers' management, and collective and political incentives. It depends on and reinforces the demobilization, demoralization, and depoliticization of the working class, not heightened communist and internationalist consciousness. It reinforces capitalist values and social norms, not the self-transformation of men and women as they transform the economic foundations of society. Ultimately this bureaucratic system— and the zigzag policies of the crystallized, petty-bourgeois social caste that promotes it—come into irrepressible conflict with nationalized property itself, because this anti-working-class political course is incompatible with building socialism. And these contradictions themselves deepen the crisis, as we are witnessing today.

A variant of this system of organization of labor in the Soviet Union and Eastern Europe—against which Che polemicized with such insight—was imposed throughout the Cuban economy in the mid-1970s as the Economic Management and Planning System. It rapidly began to produce the same social and economic consequences that have been institutionalized throughout the Soviet bloc for decades. It led to a decline in communist political consciousness and revolutionary perspectives in virtually every arena of daily social and economic activity.

Alienation, cynicism, corruption, and political demoralization grew in the working class. Che's—and Fidel's—communist political perspective lost ground to those who thought building socialism was primarily a matter of administration by a talented and privileged few, and of mechanisms that would bring economic growth as an automatic process supposedly guided by skillful use of the law of value and other methods left over from capitalism.

Those who thought of workers as objects to be controlled, as incorrigible little animals capable of advancing only if tempted with a carrot or whipped by a stick, were setting more and more of the economic and social policy of Cuba. Those who, like Che and Fidel, believed in the revolutionary capacities of working people to take the organization of the economy in hand and build a socialist society—no matter what the obstacles, no matter what the odds, and to transform themselves in the process—were put on the defensive.

The party, said Castro in December 1986, started "to go to pot," and the errors, if not corrected, could have eventually proved "irreversible," leading "to a system worse than capitalism."[20]

Volunteer labor, as Castro put it, survived during this period only because it took refuge in internationalism and defense—in aid to Angola, Nicaragua, Grenada, and other countries, and in the birth of the Territorial Troop Militia in 1980 in the face of mounting imperialist military pressure following the revolutionary victories in the Caribbean and Central America.

Regardless of these weaknesses and problems, however, the party and government in Cuba remained qualitatively different from the so-called Communist parties in the rest of the workers' states; thus, a qualitatively different road out of the developing morass was possible. A revolutionary change of direction could be initiated, because a communist leadership and politicized working-class vanguard existed in Cuba. The "lame nag," as Castro labeled the Economic Management and Planning System, could be kept working for a while as a new course was charted, the fight to win a majority to a communist perspective advanced, and a revolutionary replacement for the "lame nag" conquered.

TWENTY-FIVE years ago, Che argued that if economic planning and the organization of the working class are not designed to reinforce communist consciousness at every step rather than undermine it, then the revolution winds up in a blind alley.

"After having traveled a long distance with many crossroads," Che said, "it is hard to figure out just where you took the wrong turn. Meanwhile, the economic foundation that has been laid has done its work of undermining the development of consciousness."[21] Che not only argued this communist perspective, he tried to implement it through the budgetary finance system he pioneered in Cuba.[22] He sought to advance it by championing and organizing schools where workers could improve skills, habits of attention and study, and political self-confidence.

But Che's program for the organization of the economy and the revolutionary leadership of the working class was never tried broadly enough in Cuba to test it. Leaders responsible for other important sectors of the economy could not be convinced of the political and economic perspectives on which the budgetary finance system was based. Yet, as Castro emphasized in his October 1987 speech marking the twentieth anniversary of Guevara's death, without Che's perspectives "communism cannot be built."[23]

Che did not waste his time or energy answering the hollow breast-beating of those who loudly proclaim that a reformed capitalism is the hope of humanity. He pointed out how the course of modern history offered ample proof of the kind of horrors capitalism will bring.

CHE JOINED the real debate of our time. He took up the challenge of how imperialism can be defeated and how workers and farmers can firmly establish their political power. He joined the issue of how socialist construction can be advanced along the road toward communism. If his answers seemed utopian to some when he offered them, it was only because a version of the road defended by the privileged bureaucracy and their technicians in the Soviet Union and Eastern Europe still seemed a possible way toward socialism.

Today the burden of proof lies not with Che and Fidel, but with those who defend the political course that led to the social crises tearing apart the parties and rocking the bureaucratic castes in the Soviet Union and Eastern Europe.

The practical relevance of Che's contributions, as well as their place in the continuity of scientific socialism, can be more accurately gauged today in the context of Cuba's rectification process and these deepening crises.

"Many wonder what factors have led some socialist processes to a disastrous state," Castro noted October 1, 1989. "Someday it will be clear and there will be those who explain what this has to do with the methods used in the construction of socialism, which were actually capitalist methods. Unfortunately we were affected by this virus, thanks to some people, supposedly very theoretically knowledgeable, but who forgot the true path, the really revolutionary path to build socialism. The issue is whether you do or don't believe in people."[24]

The working people of Cuba, in whom Che had such confidence and with whom he identified blood and bone, are saving him from the fate of being redrawn as a new but still two-dimensional portrait, a new but equally sentimental and liberal icon on a wall. Through their continuing advances, and those of hundreds of millions like them, Che can and will be restored to his true historical dimensions.

In Defense of Socialism

FOUR SPEECHES ON THE 30TH ANNIVERSARY OF THE CUBAN REVOLUTION

by Fidel Castro

Fidel Castro argues that not only is economic and social progress possible without the dog-eat-dog competition of capitalism but that socialism is the only way forward for humanity. Castro also discusses Cuba's role in advancing the struggle against apartheid in Africa. 142 pp., $13.95

Cuba's Rectification Process

Two speeches by Fidel Castro reorienting the Cuban revolution toward the path championed by Che Guevara. In *New International* no. 6, $10.00

'Cuba Will Never Adopt Capitalist Methods'

by Fidel Castro

Cuba's rectification process and the historic victory in Angola over apartheid's army. 30 pp., $3.00

Building Socialism in Cuba

FIDEL CASTRO SPEECHES, VOLUME 2

Speeches spanning more than two decades trace the fight of the revolutionary vanguard to deepen the proletarian course of the Cuban revolution. 367 pp., $20.95

THE EASTERN AIRLINES STRIKE

ACCOMPLISHMENTS OF THE RANK-AND-FILE MACHINISTS
by Ernie Mailhot
Judy Stranahan
and Jack Barnes

The story of the 22-month strike—spearheaded by rank-and-file members of the International Association of Machinists—that defeated the attempt to turn Eastern, one of the world's largest carriers, into a profitable nonunion airline.
91 pp., plus 16 pp. photos. $9.95

NEW COLLECTION

TRADE UNIONS IN THE EPOCH OF IMPERIALIST DECAY
by Leon Trotsky

TRADE UNIONS: THEIR PAST, PRESENT, AND FUTURE

by Karl Marx

Two historic leaders of the revolutionary workers' movement discuss the tasks of trade unions under capitalism and their place in workers' fight for economic justice and political power.
156 pp., $14.95

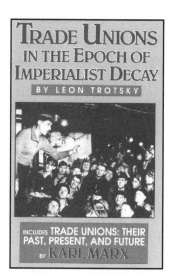

(Pathfinder)

SEE PAGE 2 FOR DISTRIBUTORS

CHE'S CONTRIBUTION
TO THE CUBAN ECONOMY

by Carlos Rafael Rodríguez

COMRADES, I would first like to thank Comrade Marcos[1] for the opportunity he has given me to meet with what might be called the leading body of this ministry, its core. It is not this body alone that is important, of course; for us, the workers are the decisive force. But this body is responsible for putting into practice the ideas of the leadership of the party and government and, above all, the ideas of the ministry.

Marcos has urged me to discuss Che's economic thought, since this year is the twentieth anniversary of Che's death and, moreover, since there are a number of comrades here who worked directly with Che. At first I was reluctant to do so. Given the amount of work we all have, it's difficult to make a systematic review of the whole body of important ideas developed by Che on how to direct the country's economy. And I did not want to come before you and take on a task that at the time seemed beyond my capacity.

But a few days ago I remembered that among the books I had received recently—which, like many others books, I had not yet had the chance to read—was the one that received the Casa de las Américas prize. The prize this year was given to a book I had taken a look at but hadn't gotten very far into—a book on Che Guevara by a studious young Cuban, Carlos Tablada.[2] It occurred to me that I should see if this book might be of any help

---

This article appeared in the May-June 1988 issue of Cuba Socialista. *It is based on a speech given at a conference of the Ministry of Basic Industry in Havana, July 21, 1987. Carlos Rafael Rodríguez is a member of the Political Bureau of the Communist Party of Cuba and a vice president of the Council of State.*

ENDNOTES FOR THIS ARTICLE BEGIN ON PAGE 183.

to me. And I can tell you that I'm very grateful for that book this afternoon. Without it, I would not have been able to come and tell Marcos that I was minimally prepared, so to speak, to share with the comrades some thoughts on Ernesto Che Guevara's contribution to problems of the national economy. I say "minimally prepared" since Che's thought has so many aspects that it's impossible to take them all up at one time. To delve into each of the many points made by Che on economic questions would require more attention than I can give to the topic and more time than you have available.

Nevertheless, the best homage that can be rendered to Che in this twentieth anniversary year by those of us who in one way or another are responsible for economic matters is to review a small part of his vast contributions to the development of the Cuban economy. These are contributions both in the field of theory as well as—and principally—in the field of practice.

Che has left a permanent imprint on our nation's industry, as he has on everything in our country. But Che was particularly linked to industry, primarily our basic industry. He was both a participant and, in large part, the driving force in the creation of our basic industry.

Marcos was telling me that like all Cubans, you here in particular preserve Che's example as something to be emulated. I believe we should all see him this way: as an example for those who are leaders and for those who are led. Recently—many of you probably saw it—there was a broadcast once again of one of the most beautiful things Cuban television has done: recollections of Che by ordinary workers who in one way or another experienced his admirable example. It is a moving documentary. One does not tire of seeing the reaction—both emotional and thoughtful—of workers who managed to grasp the essence of Che Guevara's example.

That example is priceless for us. For as Fidel said recently, we are not only engaged in a permanent battle to rectify errors—permanent because errors reproduce themselves and new errors are always cropping up, which is inevitable until we reach a state of perfection, something we have not yet attained—but we are now also part of a movement of new ideas and new initiatives.

That is why I would like, in all modesty and humility, to share with you some thoughts on Che's contributions, above all as they relate to the immediate reality we are living through.

I WILL TOUCH ON—although I won't develop it to any great extent—Che's main theoretical contribution on what is called the transition period. That is, the period in which, while slowly leaving capitalism behind, we are building socialism as fast as we can and drawing nearer to communist society—from which, in my opinion, we are still a long way off. This main contribution I am speaking of is undoubtedly Che's budgetary finance system of economic management.

This is not the system we are using today. But among the ideas on the budgetary finance system of economic management postulated by Che are some extremely timely ideas for what we are doing today. And with regard to the economic accounting system[3]—the system we use today, the one Che was so critical of—I would say that if we do not put many of Che's ideas into practice in this system, then we will not be able to move forward. A symbiosis is necessary.

Looking back, the budgetary finance system appears to us to be a contribution of exceptional value. We would not say—and you are well aware of this—that Che created the budgetary finance system. It came from the socialist countries. In the Soviet Union itself for a time, the budgetary finance system regulated many aspects of the economy. But what Che did was work to apply it to a country that was at the same time developing its economy and building socialism, a particular condition of the Cuban economy that we still confront.

Much has been written abroad—even whole books—about differences of opinion Che may have had with one or another comrade, and I in particular have been singled out. I am proud to be able to say that while we did have some differences, we always viewed things identically with regard to fundamental economic questions. We worked together, along with other comrades, to impose a little order in the Cuban economy, to attain the maximum efficiency in the Cuban economy, and to establish something that is essential—whatever one's starting point: and that is implementation of controls over the economy.

The budgetary finance system was based, first and foremost,

on use of the most advanced accounting procedures and a very modern conception—I would say it anticipated the future—of the use of computers. In this field, with his customary sweeping vision, Che was far ahead of his time in understanding how much could be done with the use of computers, which were just then emerging. He saw how they could be used to provide valuable assistance in all aspects of economic control. Strict accounting, along with widespread use of computers, was the basis of the budgetary finance system he developed.

This also went hand in hand with a very clear conception of the role of planning as a permanent instrument of the economy. Naturally, together with planning, Che proposed the centralization of budgeting as a fundamental instrument to counter the economic accounting system—a system that gives greater autonomy in budgeting to the individual enterprises. Che proposed that enterprises have no special bank accounts of their own, and that instead a centralized joint account regulate the finances of all enterprises as an economic whole.

In proposing this, Che started from the efficiency attained by the big enterprises and consortiums that the multinationals of our day had already started to become—an economic efficiency that would permit managing a conglomerate of dissimilar enterprises as though they were a single budgetary entity. Starting from the idea that socialism is better able than capitalism to direct economic centralization—which is true—Che drew the conclusion that the country's entire economy could be administered as a single enterprise, with a single joint bank account, with allocation of funds in accordance with the specific requirements of each enterprise.

Such a system would take into account—as we must—that socialism gives us the possibility to maintain, if necessary, an enterprise that permanently runs a deficit, an enterprise making products that from an economic point of view do not seem "profitable." If consideration is given solely to so-called profitability—which Che rejected (we'll come back to this)—then the production of these branches could be regarded as negative. That is, after the structure of wages is taken into account, costs might be greater than income.

But if the product made by that enterprise is a necessary one, socialism gives us a possibility that we must learn how to take advantage of. It enables us to permit enterprises that are seemingly unprofitable—we will use this term—to continue producing. This is made possible by the fact that other enterprises run at a profit and turn their funds over to the centralized state budget. These funds can then be reallocated to money-losing enterprises, permitting them to continue operating.

All this takes place under the principle of implementing economic controls. As we will see later in greater detail, Che believed this principle to be exceptionally important—a view we continue to share.

I have no intention, as I said earlier, of taking time to assess the budgetary finance system. I'm not going to take it up; we have a different system today. I would just like to make the following point:

Is the budgetary finance system more progressive than the system of economic accounting? I believe it belongs more to the future. The budgetary finance system is closer to the way the society of the future will have to be organized. But this is only a hypothesis, referring to a somewhat distant future, to the communist future.

I begin from the point of view—and this is what has led us to accept the deficiencies and shortcomings that stem from the economic accounting system—that the budgetary finance system demands conditions and possibilities we cannot attain, either in the medium term or even in the more distant future. If we were convinced that the budgetary finance system could be put into practice in the coming years, we would defend it to the death because it is based on forms of economic controls that are closer to communism. That is obvious. It is a leap like the one proposed by Karl Marx, from capitalism to an advanced socialism. As everyone knows, we have not made that leap. Not even the Soviet Union has done so.

HAVING SAID THIS, let us turn to something the two systems agree on. Remember that for Che planning, as opposed to the market, is the feature that defines socialist society. And planning is very important in both systems, including in the way we today conceive of the economic accounting system. Without planning there cannot be socialism. Planning enables us to allocate resources where they are needed. Therefore central-ized planning must exist—as we hold today in the development of our system.

Comrade Fidel has quite correctly stressed the need to main-tain centralization of the economy in its fundamental aspects. That means, above all, centralization in the selection, alloca-tion, and implementation of the national economy's plan for investment. It is not always true that what is good for a given enterprise is good for the economy as a whole. This is an axiom on which we agree.

The idea that what is good for an enterprise is good for the economy is only partially true. The enterprise is a producer of resources, a supplier of resources. If it works well it obviously must be working for the benefit of the economy. But in order for the enterprise to work for the benefit of the economy, the enterprise's plan, its investments, even the assortment of its products—and this is something Comrade Fidel particularly stresses—must be decided, in their fundamentals, in a centralized way.

If we were to let an enterprise produce whatever it wanted, whatever might be most advantageous to it economically, then we would commit grave errors. This reality has been very care-fully taken into account in a study assessing the conditions in which the enterprise of the future will function in our coun-try—a study being carried out under the leadership of Comrade Marcos by a group of comrades, some of whom are here as directors of enterprises. That I know for a fact.

A QUESTION IS being posed today that is related to what we are discussing. It is being debated today above all in Soviet circles, but it has more repercussions here in Cuba. Che took up this question, and for that reason I want to say something about it now. It has to do with the New Economic Policy drawn up by Lenin and put into practice from 1921 to 1923. At issue above all is whether or not the NEP is a strategic question—and a majority of socialist specialists at this moment seem to lean toward saying it is. Che did not think so.[4]

After a careful analysis of Lenin's writings, Che concluded that the NEP was more a tactical than a strategic conception. This is a question we ourselves will have to discuss in the future. It is not at the center of our problems, but it is an additional element we have to think about when we consider the economy as a whole.

Che emphasized that the NEP represented a step backward. To be sure, in the history of the Soviet Union it did represent a step backward with respect to what immediately preceded it. You remember that circumstances relating to the Soviet Union's defense had led the Bolshevik Party leadership to adopt what was called war communism, which was an acceleration of socialism toward elements of communism. In 1921 Lenin understood that it would be very difficult to reach communism along this road, that they had to take a step backward. That step backward was the New Economic Policy.

The New Economic Policy was based fundamentally on the economic accounting system. There is a quote from Lenin that is very clear on this: "The transfer of state enterprises to the so-called profit basis is inevitably and inseparably connected with the New Economic Policy."[5] That is, the New Economic Policy was based on taking maximum advantage of the capacity of the individual enterprise, under the conditions of the Soviet Union's economic backwardness at the time. The civil war had created an economic situation in which the working class had declined both qualitatively and quantitatively.*

We have to think about the following question, as a fundamental element for the future: How long will economic accounting endure as a system for managing the economy? We

* Leadership by the working class is spoken of and, to be sure, there was always leadership by the working class in the Soviet Union. But why is this? Because the Bolshevik Party leadership under Lenin viewed the working class as the key element in leading the country economically and politically. Not because the working class was the majority of society, as Marx had foreseen for the Germany of his day and afterward. At the time, in 1921, the working class had become a very small minority under the specific conditions of Soviet Russia. But despite all that, under the leadership of the Communist Party, the revolution had as its guide the revolutionary thought of the working class, under the guarantee of Lenin and the group of comrades around him in the central leadership of the Communist Party (Bolshevik), as the Communist Party of the Soviet Union was then called.—*CRR*

cannot foresee it now, but this surely will not be the system that
guides us when we enter the final phase approaching communist society—a time I think is still a long way off. For now, given
the specific conditions of our country—our economic backwardness, our political backwardness (despite the enormous
qualitative leaps our working class and our people have taken in
the field of politics), our backward conceptions derived from
our backward situation—we can employ economic accounting
as a guide in our present economic situation.

Another key element we have to consider in analyzing Che's
ideas is the polemic that took place in the early days of the
revolution between Che and those who at the time appeared to
be the main defenders of economic accounting and the law of
value. I would say the following: The majority of Che's contributions, or rather the totality of Che's contributions—which were
the majority of the contributions in that period on the budgetary finance system—had an extraordinary originality. If you
want to study the economic thought of Che Guevara, I would
advise you above all to examine the polemic that took place
between Che and Charles Bettelheim, a member at the time of
the French Communist Party who in the early days was helping
us in the sphere of planning. Here are Che's greatest contributions regarding the law of value.[6]

This exchange is important from the theoretical point of view
and from the point of view of analyzing the strategic fundamentals of the budgetary finance system.

I want to take up just one element from that exchange. Che
did not pose elimination of the law of value as an absolute. It is
worthwhile to recall this, since we acknowledge that the law of
value continues to operate and has certain effects. What Che
said was that the law of value could not be the guiding principle
of economic activity. He said that as a result of the conditions
created by socialism we are able to manipulate the law of value,
to use it to benefit socialism. I think this is important.

The issue is not absolute defense of the law of value, of the
inevitability of the market—although some defenders of economic accounting during that period held such a view. At issue

is controlled utilization of the law of value, taking into account the circumstances imposed by Cuba's current economic reality and historical conditions.

These conditions force us to do things as simple as, for example, acknowledging the commodity category for relations between enterprises. This was rejected by Che. To be sure, we could do away with the category of commodity and view the product simply as one element of exchange within one big enterprise, the state. But that, in our opinion, leads to even greater difficulties than if the products are considered commodities to be bought and sold by the enterprises.

But in acknowledging the continuing applicability of the commodity category, we do not accept the market as the main factor of the economy. Among Cuban defenders of the economic accounting system there is a current that goes to the extreme of viewing the market as the great arbiter of the national economy, as the organizer of the national economy. It is not necessary to hold such a viewpoint, which, in our opinion, is false and leads even to more errors than if we were to put the other system into effect. It is not necessary to defend this thesis in order to defend the economic accounting system as the appropriate means to utilize our resources in this stage of the revolution.

We cannot accept the market as the permanent arbiter of the economy. Because if we accept the market we accept with it the anarchy that the so-called free market introduces into the economy. Under the impact of the law of value, the market and the law of value act to correct unequal distributions of wealth among enterprises; this is accomplished through the law of the market and of prices, but at a tremendous cost in resources.

If we examine our economy critically, we will see that we still have not made full use of the advantages socialism gives us for organizing it. That is a fact. We speak of the inefficiency of capitalism. It's true that capitalism is inefficient, in the sense that its efficiency comes from bankrupting some enterprises and businessmen for the benefit of others. And it's a fact that socialism can be more organized, more orderly, more coherent. But we do not yet have a socialism that is either organized, orderly, or coherent! We are still today more inefficient than a well-organized capitalist society would be. We still do not have the organization, the level of organization—we'll talk more about this later—that socialism enables us to have.

So when we talk about the utilization of the commodity category, we are referring to relative utilization of the market. We utilize the market. Together with products that have only a regulated market—like the ration-book market in our country—there are products that are sold on what we call the parallel market.[7] The parallel market takes the law of supply and demand into account in setting the price of products. But it is not an independent market in which the law of supply and demand prevails absolutely. It is a market in which the leadership of the country uses, in a regulated way, the possibilities offered by the law of supply and demand to set prices that approach what would be market prices if a market existed. Here we direct the market, we are not subordinate to it. Not subordinating ourselves to the market is one of the permanent elements in our conception of how to apply the economic accounting system.

That is why we can accept the idea that Che put in the following words: "We consider the law of value to be partially operative because remnants of the commodity society still exist."[8] There is an additional sentence by Che that we cannot accept, however, namely: "We reject the existence of the *commodity* category in relations among state enterprises."[9] This we do not accept; it is not what prevails in our system. But the first statement, "We consider the law of value to be partially operative," is part of what we are applying.

And we have to acknowledge the truth of Che's dictum: "The law of value and the plan are two terms linked by a contradiction."[10]

IN REALITY the plan is contradictory to utilizing the market and, consequently, to utilizing the law of value. The plan becomes more reconcilable with utilizing the market and the law of value when the law of value is interpreted as partially operative—that is, when we utilize it rather than allowing it to conquer us. An example of this was when we established the market as an element steered by the country's economic leadership bodies.

What do we find when we examine Che's ideas in this regard?

In the first years Che worked on the economy with the enthusiasm all of us had then, with his enormous capacity to keep the future in view. Che himself was a communist. And we should understand that we are not using the term *communist* here to refer to a member of a party. I'm talking about a man capable of living in a communist society, which is something quite different.

Developing communist consciousness

However, Che let himself be carried away by an idea that was incorrect in my opinion, and I must say this in all honesty. Che held the view that it was possible in the short term to attain the level of consciousness of a communist society, that the development of consciousness could be speeded up. He believed that this could be done in the framework of the political transition then under way in Cuba—in the imperfect socialist society in which we were beginning to build socialism in 1959, 1960, and 1961. That's why he proposed eliminating in the most vigorous way possible the old categories, principally the law of value.

So if I may say something on this, I'd like to repeat a sentence from Lenin that should be taken into account, and that corresponds to what we are doing. "Relying on firmness of convictions, loyalty, and other splendid moral qualities is anything but a serious attitude in politics," Lenin pointed out. "A few people may be endowed with splendid moral qualities, but historical issues are decided by vast masses, which, if the few do not suit them, may at times treat them none too politely."[11] In other words, confidence should be accompanied by controls.

There is something we must insist on: we must not lack confidence in man. Fidel has often insisted on this.

We continually see errors, weaknesses, incorrect actions by people who we thought were representatives of this society. But we cannot let ourselves fall prey to a lack of confidence. We have to continue placing confidence in human beings, in the possibility of their perfectibility. The Germans have a saying, one I like very much, to the effect that "trust is good, but a watchful eye is better." Alongside confidence, controls.

Fidel's call for confidence comes at a moment when we are in a battle for the rectification of errors—not a campaign but a battle to rectify errors. It is a battle to examine and monitor all aspects of national life, and to do so from the grass-roots level. Not just through mechanisms of the party, which are useful to the highest degree as a system of controls. Not only through financial mechanisms, which are an essential element in checking up on things. And not just through accounting, which is also an indispensable element. But also with the participation of the masses, of the workers in the factories, in administrative centers, in education, in the cooperatives, in the state production units.

In short, we want to move toward a stage where Che will be totally present. Now Che is present, but I would say only partially present. We have chosen a system for managing the economy that is different from what he advocated, but not so different as is supposed, as is sometimes said.

One of the biggest heresies committed in this country was to suppose that what we were doing from 1967 to 1970—the lack of economic controls that prevailed in those years—could be carried out, as some did, in the name of Che Guevara. That was the most unjust, the most antihistorical, the most, I'd say . . . I was going to use a stronger term, but I'll limit myself to the word "lamentable." That system of total lack of controls carried out in the name of Che, invoking Che, had nothing at all to do with Che. I remember that some of our institutions brought out pamphlets containing what was alleged to be the thought of Che Guevara, but which in reality was the *mutilated* thought of Che Guevara.

LET US now meet Che on common ground.

I'm going to quote something he said, to show how close it comes to our present conceptions. Che was one of the first to state: "Communism is a phenomenon of consciousness and not solely a phenomenon of production. We cannot attain communism if man is not conscious."

He continued: "In our view communism is a phenomenon of consciousness and not solely a phenomenon of production. We cannot arrive at communism through the simple mechanical accumulation of quantities of goods made available to the people."[12]

I think that gets to the heart of our present position. We want to arrive at communist society as quickly as possible; some see it as being closer than others. How one judges the matter depends on a number of factors including human temperament, not just experience.

But there is one thing we must be firm on. It is true that society cannot be communist before we arrive at communism—society, *society*. But it is also true that society will not become communist if we simply wait for the arrival of communism—that is, if we wait for an abundance of goods to produce the type of man needed by that society.

Both things are true. We cannot have a communist society as long as there is a socialist distribution of work. And as long as we have a socialist distribution of the results of work, we will have a socialist society. Any attempt to alter these principles would be premature and in vain.

Then how will we arrive at communism? To get to communism we have to work for communism starting from where we are today. Che held this correct position, as has Fidel from the very beginning. We also adhere to it. And when I say "we," I mean Cuban society as a whole, or at least thousands of people in Cuban society. We consider each day a battle for communism, each day a battle for consciousness. It is not possible yet to have a communist society. But there can indeed be many communists prior to reaching a communist system.

In reality we have to increase our efforts—and we are still far from having done this successfully—to have all party members prepared to work at keeping socialist society from dominating us. Socialist society, as Marx said in the *Critique of the Gotha Program,* is a society ruled by bourgeois principles of distribution. It is ruled that way because we have no other choice. If we tried to rule it by communist principles of distribution we would be making a serious error; society as a whole is not ready for this.

But if we allow bourgeois principles to prevail over our intention of building socialism and transforming it into communism, if we allow bourgeois principles to overwhelm us and become the dominant ones in this society, then instead of working for communism we will be working for the return of capitalism. To the degree we allow bourgeois principles to become ideologically dominant—and this is something very important to understand—we will be retreating from the road to communism, we will be going backward.

On the other hand, if we make each day a battle to deepen

workers' consciousness of egalitarian distribution, of a more equitable distribution; if workers become prepared to see this sort of society prevail—and communists must be the first in this—we will then be taking big steps toward communism.

Che said, "We have always stressed this dual aspect of the construction of socialism. Building socialism is neither a matter of work alone, nor of consciousness alone." This is very important. It's not just work, it's not just a greater production of goods, and it's not just consciousness. If we were to dedicate ourselves to advancing consciousness without taking into account efficiency at work, we would not be building a communist society, we would be building a society that was ideologically communist but without communism. And if we dedicate ourselves to work, to produce more, without developing consciousness, we will build a society of communist abundance but on noncommunist principles. The men who live in it will not be capable of taking advantage of the abundance to establish a communist society.

And Che added: "Building socialism is neither a matter of work alone, nor of consciousness alone. It combines work and consciousness—expanding the production of material goods through work, and developing consciousness. Emulation has to fulfill both of these goals, both of these functions."[13]

With regard to this point, I'd like to refer to something Fidel said at the First Congress of our party [in 1975] that reflects how we guide ourselves.

Fidel said: "Under socialism, no system can substitute for politics, for ideology, for people's consciousness. The factors that determine efficiency in a capitalist economy are different and can never exist under socialism. Fundamental and decisive under socialism are the political aspect, the ideological aspect, and the moral aspect."[14]

WE HAVE TO take this into account as a permanent element in our approach to the battle we are carrying out. This is above all a battle in which economic efficiency is linked to raising the moral level of our society. And we cannot raise the moral level as if we were in a vacuum. We have to take into account society as it is, the elements within it that tend to corrupt us, that tend to pull us backward. Not just the elements of distribution but also elements of conduct that still exist in society.

Marx said something very interesting in this regard: "But these defects are inevitable in the first phase of communist society"—that is, in the socialist phase, which is what we have— "as it is when it has just emerged after prolonged birth pangs from capitalist society. Justice can never be higher than the economic structure of society and the cultural development thereby determined."[15]

In other words, justice is on the one hand a reflection of the economic structure, which we help advance to the degree that we seek to produce more, better, with higher quality, and with greater efficiency; on the other hand, justice is a reflection of the moral behavior that helps adjust this society toward the society we are advancing to.

And what is needed for that? I would like to cite something Che said that we might mention later, in almost any context. In fact, later we will take up several things he said, because they are very useful today for carrying out our day-to-day work.

Che said, very categorically: "Without controls we cannot build socialism."[16] That is, if we do not put controls at the center of our activity, we will not be able to build socialism. Why? "The problem is that people are not perfect, far from it. We have to improve systems of controls to detect the very first infraction, because the first one leads to all the others."[17]

Notice how clearly he, a communist, who was out ahead of society as a whole, was aware of its faults and errors. Che had immense faith in man, immense faith in man's capabilities; he had confidence in man in all elements of daily life, in voluntary work, in the work of the factory. He always had confidence in the human being. And he said: "People might be very good the first time. But when, through indiscipline, they commit the error of taking something for personal use, intending to replace it in two or three days, this can then spread to the point of their becoming thieves, becoming traitors, falling increasingly into crime."[18]

That is the kind of person we all are. We do not consider ourselves immune from this type of error. And the only way we have of avoiding it is to struggle against the evil inside ourselves, against the survival of the past; and to supervise and hold accountable those around us, to prevent the first mistake from leading to a second. Because it is easy to correct the first mistake, difficult to correct the second, and impossible to correct the mistakes when they become part of a person's behavior. We have to fight such conduct, which we still have signs of in our society every day. We ourselves have to fight it, through our struggle against our own weaknesses. And socialism as a whole has to fight it with collective controls, above and beyond those exercised by official bodies of review and supervision.

Lᴇᴛ ᴜs ᴛᴜʀɴ to another aspect of our daily work: the form in which wages are paid and the system by which they are determined. This is interesting because it explains a great deal about ideas of Che that are useful in their essence, even though in practice we have chosen not to apply them.

The wage system established by Che started from work completed in a given amount of time, with bonuses for surpassing the norm in quantity, in quality, and—I call attention to this— for the level of skill attained by the individual worker, both administrative and technical workers. Above all, pay was based on the amount of time worked.

What is the significance of this? I remember, and I'm sure several of you also remember, those of you who are closer to my age—there are many younger people here who may have read about this—that in those early years Fidel, who was occupied with other activities, handed direction of the economy over to a body called the Economic Commission of the National Directorate. It was made up of Che, Comrade Dorticós, and myself.[19] Augusto Martínez Sánchez, who was then the minister of labor, participated actively in the discussion we had on wages. And I remember that the three of us on the commission finally resolved all the questions brought up in that discussion.

There was one thing Che was especially concerned about in establishing awards and bonuses. He was concerned that no matter how much the individual effort of a worker surpassed the norm, no worker in the third, fourth, fifth, or sixth category would receive in wages and bonuses a higher income than a worker in the next higher category.

It's important to remember this, because it gives us an idea of something in Che's conception that I think relates to *that specific time*. (I'm not trying to define anything with these words, but I do think some of Che's ideas are based on the circumstances of *that specific time*.) Because at that time there was a total lack of technical training in our working class. We had hardly any technicians. Capitalism had left us a small number, and we were making use of them. But in general we were improvising with technicians, improvising with machinists, improvising with milling-machine operators—in short, with every technician in the national economy.

Che said the following, which I agree with wholeheartedly: If we arrange things so that someone who is studying to become a machinist, or who might study to become a machinist, takes a job in a category immediately below that of a machinist and makes more money than he would make as a machinist, without actually becoming one—then we would be undercutting our effort to encourage study and the attainment of skills. That is true. It had a basis in fact. And, as you remember, it was the point of view that prevailed.

I saw things a little differently. We were fighting to encourage layers in our society to attain higher skills and to create the conditions so that someone who was not a machinist would become one and, as a machinist in category C, would make more than a machinist in category A. While we were doing this, however, for a long time we were wasting an amount of effort and work that people were not prepared to carry out unless we offered possibilities for higher wage earnings. I could have been wrong. But I tell you this clearly and in all honesty, so you can understand the two positions.

We adopted Che's position and it had a very important effect: spreading throughout the working class the idea of attaining a higher job category through your own effort to increase your skill level. That is, it was not only physical effort alone that resulted in a higher income. You could get a higher wage through physical effort. But you could also do it through an effort directed at improving the quality of your labor, through the transition to a higher level of work attained by raising your technical skills.

And here we come to an interesting idea. At that moment

there emerged what was later called the "historic wage"—at the time we called it the "plus." We all felt the "plus" was a necessity—I don't know if I have Che's words here, but he spoke of this very concretely.

We had a layer of workers who, through union struggles and great effort, had managed to wrest a number of concessions from the bosses in the period prior to the revolution. Among these concessions were wage levels that, in the framework of the society in which we were beginning to build socialism, could not be given to all workers. These wages were higher than the median wage we were able to pay for these jobs. Cutting back on these wages, however, would have had negative consequences. It would have meant that some workers—those who by their efforts and the efforts of their unions had won wage levels higher than those we were able to pay—would have been forced to give up wages they had been receiving since before the revolution. We all understood this, as Che did immediately. That's how the "plus" emerged, was accepted, and, after some time, became what we now call the "historic wage."

What did Che say about this? What was agreed to at the time? It was agreed that the "plus" would be the maximum a worker surpassing the norm could make in wages. In other words, if a worker surpassed the norm, once he reached the "historic wage," his bonus could go no higher. For example, if there are workers making [the historic wage of] 270 pesos and another worker alongside them is being paid 275 pesos, because of his hard work, then we are making a mistake. This applies more generally as well. So that's how we set the level, taking the "historic wage" as the highest level. That is important.

Now let us turn to the wage system. The wage system is linked to Che's efforts. We complain about the great number of job categories in our country. And the truth is there are many more job categories than there would be if things were better organized. The fundamental problem is overly rigid job classifications.

But I can assure you that in the years 1962-63, when we began to study these problems, there was total anarchy with regard to wages. This stemmed from a number of sources. First, from the anarchy of capitalism, and from the fact that each capitalist had his own wage scale. And second, from the fact that each union had its own history of struggle, with the result that some were able to obtain advantages not obtained by others, despite belonging to the same union movement. So when this wage anarchy was reduced to the eight categories we established at the time, it represented an enormously important step, enormously important.

Some other time we can examine whether there should be eight, six, four, or five job categories. I say that we can look into that another time, together with some specialists. That is a problem we don't have to take up today, because we are looking at Che's contribution to the national economy. But the organization of the wage system in this form was one of his most serious and solid contributions. It lasted the whole first period of the revolution.

Che combined this form of wage organization with one of his essential concepts in the struggle to advance toward communism. This is very important, because it is still part of our conception today. He said that we had to struggle daily to convert work from something disagreeable into a "moral necessity."[20] Marx called work a "prime necessity."[21] We could say that a "prime necessity" is virtually the same as a "moral necessity," thereby uniting Marx and Che in these categories that are similar when you analyze them in depth. Work—and this is something Che said many times—is a *social duty*. Fidel too has continually stressed this since the earliest days of the revolution. And this battle is more important for us today than ever.

Of all the elements we have lost in recent years, one of the most harmful has been the elimination of the conception of work as a social duty. This conception fell victim to the anarchy introduced into our social relations by improper use of the system of planning and management we had adopted; by poor use of what we had approved, of things that could have been very useful had we applied them well. This is one of the things we have to study; in fact, it is something that appears continually in studies presented by the commission established for this purpose.

The basis of our society, as Fidel has said, began imperceptibly to become, without our being aware of it, the automatic operation of economic mechanisms. That is, the idea emerged that economic mechanisms could by themselves, without political work, resolve the problem of harmonizing individual interests with collective interests. Another idea that began to take hold was that the group interests of those in an individual workplace or anywhere else expressed the interests of society as a whole. These are erroneous ideas. As I said before, it is not always true that individual interests coincide with the interests of society. To make sure they do—to assure, for example, that the interests of an enterprise or a factory do not begin to contradict the interests of society—the society as a whole has to keep watch on the interests both of individuals and institutions.

So starting from that point of view, from the understanding that those in any particular enterprise or institution cannot themselves resolve problems that correspond to society as a whole, several things become clear: we should not try to convert the mechanisms into something automatic; we should not try to use the mechanisms automatically; and we should not believe that mechanisms by themselves will lead to bettering the nation. It is possible that the mechanism by itself might lead only to bettering a group of individuals. Whether the group is larger or smaller is not decisive. What is decisive is bettering the nation as a whole.

Starting from the other point of view, which we are now rejecting, you arrive at the conclusion that the more money the individual makes the better he will feel, the more useful he will be to society, and the more he will produce. We reached a situation of individual activity without any regulation or controls. The ones making more money were not necessarily those producing more, but rather those who appeared to be producing more or those who the administrators allowed to make more money, or those to whom the administrators give the privilege of making more. What we end up with are the distortions that have been pointed out through the enormous process of criticism and reassessment that has taken place throughout the country.

If we start from the point of view of work as a social duty, we do not eliminate the fact that he who produces more receives more. We do not eliminate the *socialist* principle of remuneration, but we do condition it with a specific conception of work. It's clear we won't reach this overnight! For the reasons Che noted, because we're not perfect; we are perfectible but not perfect. We can also be made imperfect, that is, we can be corrupted.

We start from the point of view that we must give more to those who work harder. But even those who receive more because of their good work—even a canecutter who makes more than a doctor—must be conscious that he is not working only to make more money. He is receiving more because he works harder, but he is working because it is useful to society. We will not attain this consciousness overnight, in a month, or in a year. It takes political work, ideological work, work in raising individual and collective consciousness. It takes work in which the collectivity plays a certain role.

To move closer to the better society we aspire to, we have to make sure every worker has this in mind, as well as the director of the enterprise, the party unit in the enterprise, the trade union—in other words, the collectivity as a whole. If one part of this broad collective leadership I mentioned—I would add of course the Union of Communist Youth—if this broad collective leadership composed of the leadership of the factory, plus the party, the union, and the communist youth does not take these things into account; if instead they dedicate themselves to producing more so the workers will make more, or to the workers making more because they have produced more, forgetting the job of raising consciousness, then we will be committing a serious error, an error that will claim all of us as its victims.

Now LET'S take a look, along the same lines, at another aspect we are placing a great deal of emphasis on—the problem of quality.

What did Che say? He said: "The norm is not just quantity, it is also quality."[22] That is, he had a very clear concept, even in those early days during which everything tended toward quality not being a predominant consideration.

In the early stages of socialism, which is where we still are today, demand outstrips supply. The family's income is greater than society's capacity to produce. The reason is precisely because we are creating a distributive, socialist society where we give a job to everyone possible, and where, moreover, we are inefficient.

What happens among us? A bus may not come to a full stop. If you protest the driver says, "Take it or leave it." And if the driver goes to a store, he in turn is told, "Take it or leave it. This is all we have, don't bother looking for better quality than this." And if the man from the store goes to a restaurant, he is told the same thing, "Take it or leave it." An entire chain of "take it or leave it," as a concept, as an idea.

But this question is so important that in those initial days of the revolution—when every tendency was toward production, production at any cost—Che emphasized the centrality of the problem of quality. "The norm is not just quantity, it is also quality." If a worker has not produced "such and such an amount" of "such and such" quality, he has not fulfilled his duty to society. In other words, just meeting the quota for quantity does not fulfill a worker's social duty. From the very beginning, Che considered producing with greater quality to be an essential task of the worker.

Also of great importance is Che's conception of what the norm is. Because we tend to see the norm as an objective to be attained when in reality it is something else, as Che himself explained.

The minimum work norm is a worker's duty to society. This does not mean that each and every worker can meet the norm. In some cases there are physical handicaps and natural weaknesses that a worker cannot overcome, no matter how hard he may try. If the norm is set properly, however, it will not be something that simply requires above-average ability. It will also be a goal that every worker has a growing possibility of attaining. The worker must not see the norm as something that is unattainable, as something that can be achieved only by those who produce the most. Instead, the worker must view the norm as something that constitutes the measure of his duty to society. This is a concept that Che cherished. I have come across a number of places where Che makes this point. It turns up often.

Along these lines—on norms, and on economic controls— there is another thing Che said that we should recall, because it is extremely timely. As soon as controls fall apart, Che said, along with them the entire organizational apparatus we have put together will also fall apart. This was one of his concerns, which we will come back to later.

Why should this be of such concern to us? Because this has been one of the fundamental defects of the period we have just concluded, and it is one of the fundamental elements of the period that is opening up.

Controls and norms. Norms mean production of quality goods. But they also mean something else, and this is very important; Che said something about this too. Norms mean production at the *lowest possible cost*. We will speak about this more later on. But the point here is that he linked three things: producing more; producing with greater efficiency—that is, at the lowest possible cost; and producing with all the necessary quality. These three themes are also part of what we do today. And when we think of Che we have to think of these kinds of things. Because while Che's death was heroic and for us very dramatic, it is not only through the way he died that he left an example for Cuban society.

THIS BRINGS US to the question of incentives, a question that has been much discussed.

At this point I would like to say—because there has been a lot of talk about it—that on the question of incentives I had small differences with Che. I stress, however, *small* differences.

Our ongoing debate was above all one of proportions: how much weight should be given to moral incentives; how much to material incentives; by how much and in what way can we reduce material incentives to their minimum; and what role can education play in this. The question of the pace of acceleration was where our differences centered.

I believed that by raising the level of consciousness we could reduce the use of material incentives, of money, within our society. But I felt the pace could not be maintained at the rate that Che believed possible at that moment—I repeat, at that moment.

Che said: "We recognize [material interest] . . . and apply it in our norms of hourly work including bonuses, and wage penalties for nonfulfillment of these norms."[23] In other words, he acknowledged material interest as a fundamental element that had to be taken into account. But his starting point was the need to fight for the rapid elimination of material interest.

"In our view, direct material incentives and consciousness are contradictory terms," he said.[24] I too believe that when we analyze them deeply they are contradictory terms. But the contradiction is one we have to live with, and one that Che lived with.

Che held that we have to have an intelligent and qualitatively balanced utilization of both—of material incentives and moral incentives, of material incentives and consciousness. And here we are completely and totally in agreement.

The process, Che believed, should tend more toward the withering away than the suppression of material incentives. The announcement of a policy of moral incentives does not imply the total negation of material incentives. It is simply a matter of trying to reduce their field of action, and to do this through intense ideological work rather than by bureaucratic measures.

"We must make one thing clear," Che said. *"We do not deny the objective need for material incentives,* although we are reluctant to use them as the main lever. . . . It should not be forgotten that it comes from capitalism and is destined to die under socialism."[25]

This is something we should give a great deal of thought to; it explains a conception we can adhere to in principle without being in literal agreement with each of its expressions. The important thing is this: Material incentives will perish, consciousness is what lasts. Material incentives are what we must leave behind, consciousness is what must move to the forefront. We use material incentives because they are inevitable, not because they are better; we use them because they are inevitable.

But when the time comes—and I cannot tell you when that will be; it depends on the mobilization of the party, on public education, on education in the family, on many factors that have to do with both the collective and the individual. When the time comes that we can dispense with material incentives, there is no doubt it would be practically counterrevolutionary to continue basing ourselves on material incentives.

Material incentives, I repeat, will perish; they must be eliminated through our work. I believe these are the ideas Fidel has been expressing, that have been in the forefront of his thinking in recent times. That is, to use material incentives in a limited way while understanding that consciousness is the most important thing in the work of society as a whole.

On May 2, 1962, and I quote this from Tablada's book, Che met with some worker delegates from abroad who had attended the May Day activity in the Plaza of the Revolution. A Canadian delegate asked him—and here I quote the Canadian delegate: "What incentives will the Cubans use with the workers? Are there some incentives aimed at increasing production?" Che responded in part: "I don't know if you were at the annual meeting April 30 where we gave away forty-five houses to the best workers in each branch of industry. It turned out that forty-four were given away, because one worker declined his prize."[26]

I was present at that meeting, held at the García Lorca Theater if I remember correctly; if not, perhaps one of the comrades here can correct me. In any event, Che was the one who awarded the forty-four houses, and he bestowed extraordinary praise on the worker who declined the forty-fifth house. It might seem paradoxical, but this was in fact a way of fighting for two principles at the same time: to continue using material incentives, and to praise the fact that someone declined them. And you all know what it would be like to decline a material incentive, a house—I think I remember it was a worker in the cement industry, in Artemisa, something like that. But praising this example ahead of the other forty-four, without slighting the forty-four, without hurting those who had accepted (because Che, as you well know, had sensitivity, a tremendous spiritual fineness), without slighting the other forty-four, he called attention to the example of the one who had no desire to accept the house he had been awarded.

Let us turn to another topic—don't worry, I'm getting near the end—to the role of cost accounting.

I can talk here as though I were with family, because I know that Marcos and the comrades who direct the ministry along with him, and you the directors of enterprises, of the ministry, and the technicians, all the comrades who work here—some time ago you waged a systematic struggle to improve cost accounting. I think that is one of the things we can applaud most about this ministry. Marcos told me just now that you still had a way to go to attain this.

I remember that between the years 1967 and 1970, there was an unrelenting current that wanted to eliminate this kind of accounting. And for example, when Fidel quite correctly states that we now have accountants, we cannot forget that for many years the accountants simply disappeared. Not only did the accountants disappear but so did the account books. And not only did the account books disappear, but along with them the know-how of conducting cost accounting.

This work of reconstruction is difficult. It's easy to destroy but much harder to rebuild. It's easier to destroy a system than to build one anew. Because with the destruction of a system goes the destruction of habits and concepts. And one of the best things we had in this country—and I think this is accurate—was our system of accounting.

Wʜᴀᴛ ʜᴀᴘᴘᴇɴᴇᴅ? We destroyed that system of accounting, and we are working now to rebuild it. We must place the ideas of Comrade Ernesto Che Guevara at the heart of rebuilding this system.

Che said: "Costs concern us greatly today; we have to work on this relentlessly. When prices are kept at fixed levels, costs become our basic tool for evaluating the management of units or enterprises. And once the cost has been determined—whether figured on the basis of the overall costs of the production process, or the cost per unit of output—any administrator can quickly detect problems even of a technological character.

"These might include, for example, excessive consumption of steam; defects in the bottling machine that is perhaps ejecting too many bottle caps; a machine that might be moving the bottles before they've been filled; or an automatic scale that puts too much of a product in a container. Any of these things can be detected simply through an analysis of costs.

"This does not mean we do not still need all the types of technical controls"—Che was always very careful to try not to be misunderstood—"but simply that we need a well-executed analysis of costs, something that will enable the director of any enterprise or the administrator of any unit to master completely his area of responsibility."[27]

We are here speaking to an assembly of administrators, directors of enterprises, of groups of enterprises, and I don't think it is necessary to stress the importance of this, of cost accounting.

Che said: "Rigorous controls are needed throughout the entire organizational process. These controls begin at the base, in the production unit. They require statistics that one can feel confident are exact, as well as good habits in using statistical data. It's necessary to know how to use statistics. These are not just cold figures—although that's what they are for the majority of administrators today, with the possible exception of output figures. On the contrary, these figures contain within them an entire series of secrets that must be unveiled. Learning to interpret these secrets is the task of the day."[28]

I think this is something that can help refresh you as to the importance of such data.

As Fidel has said, figures can be deceiving. But if we have a capable team of managers and administrators in an enterprise, with an efficient accountant, a trained economist, and an enterprise director who may be a technician or an economist, either of the two—with a group of workers like this we will be able to uncover the secrets that lie behind the figures. And this is very important, because cold figures alone are of no use. That is, it's what lies *behind* those figures that must be learned by the factory administrator, by the accountant, the economist, so they can analyze the enterprise's work.

You remember the systematic analysis meetings that were held on the work of the enterprises, under Che's leadership. I think some of you took part in these a few times, I know Marcos did. An entire day of analyzing everything that occurred in a factory—from stocks of inputs, to problems of technology and finance—everything was minutely analyzed. The records of a small number of these analysis meetings have been preserved, and I recommend them as an outstanding example of how to study the functioning of an enterprise. Because this has nothing to do with one system of economic management or the other. The analytical methodology employed by Che, as a leading

administrator, to examine, to analyze, to deepen our understanding of the work of an enterprise is one of the most valuable
elements we have in the history of the Cuban economy. It
should serve as an example for all ministries to follow. I believe
this is important.

Today I think we should feel ashamed. We have 1.8 billion
pesos worth of inventory, but that's not the point. The thing to
look at is the useless inventory we have on hand. Because we
count as part of our inventory not only what is being used—this
year I think we are using 300 million pesos in inventory in the
national economy—but the inventory we have allowed to grow
for reasons of carelessness, for business reasons of always having
some stocks to fall back on, for reasons of lack of controls, for all
kinds of reasons.

WE HAVE an economic apparatus today that is qualitatively
superior to what we used to have. I remember the first group of
directors of enterprises, that is, even before the establishment of
the school for administrators you are now rebuilding—the one
at Vento, and the one in El Vedado, in the old Baldor school. It
was there, for the first time, that Che began to take up these
problems and discuss them with a group of administrative and
technical personnel, when he was beginning to become concerned about these things. But nobody knew anything, not even
us. The mistakes we made then were the result of the moment
through which we were passing. But the mistakes we have made
in recent years are mistakes of carelessness, which is something
completely different.

Che said on this point: "To conduct inventory on a scientific
basis, we also have to keep track of the stock of basic means of
production."[29] Here I think we've made a little progress, but we
have to be careful here too.

He said: "Financial discipline is one of the most important
aspects of managing an enterprise or a factory. . . . The books must
be kept up to date. This includes expenditures and income, all
questions relating to contracts—for example, a negotiated adjust-
ment concerning the delivery of a defective product. All these
things are part of financial discipline, of financial controls."[30]

And he added: "Cost must be the real barometer of the performance of an enterprise. . . . What is important is constant evaluation of the management of an enterprise, over a given period, measured by its success in lowering costs."[31]

I have mentioned all these things about financial discipline, comrades, because one might think that the budgetary finance system of managing the economy was more "benevolent" in terms of economic conduct than the economic accounting system. That is not true. I think the opposite is true.

In fact, at the beginning of the revolution the budgetary finance system of management may have provided better economic controls than the initial form of the economic accounting system.

But the important thing is to underscore the need to be intransigent. We have to be intransigent with errors. Do not overlook errors, do not assume they will correct themselves. Errors must be corrected. They have to be corrected from the top, from the middle, and from the bottom. They have to be corrected from the bottom to the top. If we don't have a demanding minister, then the deputy ministers won't be demanding, then the directors won't be demanding; if the directors aren't demanding, then the heads of production won't be demanding. And we end up with a general lack of care and rigor, which is what happened in the last few years in production in our country. A demanding attitude, controls, and continual attention—that is what's important.

Finally, comrades, I would like to say something about our approach to the question of administrative and technical personnel, the question of cadres. His approach to this question was another thing that characterized Ernesto Che Guevara's stint as minister of industry and as a leader of the nation's entire economy.

Today we are revitalizing the way we take up the question of administrative and technical personnel, of cadres. Not because we don't already have a clear approach to the matter. Raúl [Castro] has been one of the people who has complained most when we overlook this. He always refers to a document on cadres we drew up at our party's First Congress. It was not perfect, but I would say it was quite good. But we have not made use of that document, we have not applied it. That still lies ahead of us. It looked as though it would not be of much use and it turned out to be extraordinarily useful.

Today we have to begin to revitalize our approach to this question. It is a careful approach, one that seems to meet both the requirements of the ministries and the leading economic bodies, and of the directors of enterprises. It is coordinated under the watchfulness of the party, through its departments, and with the participation of the ranks. We think that continual monitoring by the workers is an essential element in our policy toward administrative and technical cadres. If we don't make provisions for the workers to participate, we'll go wrong. We are making a profound error if we think we can keep a total monopoly on the selection of such personnel from above.

Speaking of cadre selection policy, Che said the following: "When it became clear that a new social class had definitively taken command in Cuba, we also saw the great limitations that would be faced in the exercise of state power because of the conditions in which we found the state. There were no cadres to carry out the enormous number of jobs that had to be filled in the state apparatus, in the political organization, and on the entire economic front. . . .

"But with the acceleration of the process beginning with the nationalization of the U.S. enterprises and later of the large Cuban enterprises, a real hunger for administrative technicians came about. On the other hand, an urgent need was felt for production technicians because of the exodus of many who were attracted by better positions offered by the imperialist companies in other parts of Latin America or in the United States itself. While engaged in these organizational tasks, the political apparatus had to make an intense effort to provide ideological attention to the masses who had joined the revolution eager to learn."[32]

Che was trying to point out here the initial difficulties in selecting administrative and technical cadres. But we, who no longer have those initial difficulties, should be a little ashamed that we have not applied the policy on administrative and technical personnel. Especially since we've had marvellous examples of it, including the example of Che and the example he left behind in the Ministry of Industry itself.

What is the situation today? I took a look at some of the figures the other day. In the Ministry of Agriculture, in 1966-67 we had fewer than three hundred agronomists and fewer than three hundred veterinarians. And of those veterinarians, a majority would have been frightened if they had seen a bull; they were used to treating dogs and cats and didn't know there were any animals as big as bulls. Today we have thousands of technicians, thousands of engineers. We have them in every industry, thousands of technicians, thousands of engineers. We have advanced. Our agriculture of today is not what it was in 1963, 1964, and 1965. Our advances in this field resemble the athlete who has been trained but has not yet begun to run. In many sectors of industry the same thing is true. We have a whole group of people who can be put into industry to produce, but production still is not at the level that this group of people would enable us to have.

We have to come to grips with the fact that it is essential to take a correct approach to this question of cadres. We are at a moment in which cadres plus the masses, acting together, decide everything. And when I speak of cadres I'm not just speaking of the most important leaders of the revolution, I'm not just referring to the ministers and directors of enterprises. I'm also referring to middle-level cadres, to those of whom we have spoken about so much recently, to the cadre who helps keep the worker working, to the cadre who leads a brigade, to all the cadres of the country. Every cadre in the country must constantly work along the same lines.

HERE ARE some things Che mentioned continually as elements of a cadre policy.

First, setting an example. A cadre must be a man of the vanguard, he must be someone who day after day helps forge the revolutionary spirit. If you don't set an example, you can't be a leader; you have to set an example. And Che continually did so—in voluntary work, in social behavior, in the way he acted, in his modesty, in all the virtues that he modestly displayed. Although you cannot really say Che made a display of his virtues; on the contrary, they were part of him. He demanded them of himself, and he exhibited them because this was what he gave us, as an example for everyone. He never made an ostentatious show of any of these virtues. He was as modest as one could possibly be, modest even in his own virtues.

Second, raising one's educational and skill level. We should never think we have come far enough in this. It was Che who once said—and I think the day is approaching when it will be true—that we would one day have "sixth-grade illiterates." He said this when the first workers were being graduated from the sixth grade. Why? Because at that time to reach the sixth grade was a feat. It meant conquering something we could all really be proud of, because we began in this country with a million illiterates. So when the Cuban working class began to attain a sixth-grade education—and this was only the beginning—it was something extraordinary. But Che said be careful, "we have to understand that in the age of technology a sixth-grade education will be the equivalent of illiteracy."[33] And we should never forget that.

There are even middle-level technicians who can be considered illiterates, not because they are really illiterate but because the goal to be attained is much higher. That does not mean that everyone has to go to the university. That would be an error. This is an error in the Cuban family. The first thing the Cuban family thinks of when a child is born is that the child is going to be an engineer or a doctor. It never occurs to anyone to say, "This child is going to be a skilled worker"; nobody ever thinks of that. But in the revolution a skilled worker has as much dignity as a doctor or an engineer. The important thing is to perform with excellence whatever work you do. That is the most important thing, and that should be imbued in everyone.

But someone who is a skilled worker cannot rest content with that; he should work for something better, to improve himself. What Che wanted to accomplish when he set as a ceiling that a worker of a lower job category, through physical exertion, could not earn more than the next higher category of worker—was to put us all in motion toward improving ourselves, including those who had already reached the university level.

Today the university is no more than a beginning. Today science is advancing at such a pace that a scientist who does not go back to school every year or so will not really be a scientist within four years. His scientific theories will be outdated, because science is making such rapid progress that it leaves us all behind. The same is true for technicians. The technician who does not adjust daily, yearly to the rhythm of the new machines will be of less use in his technological work.

And finally, comrades, austerity—austerity in all our conduct.

We have recently seen some dramatic examples of a lack of austerity. Among us, Che was the exceptional example of austerity in daily conduct, down to the way he dressed. To be sure, not everyone is going to be as original as Che in his manner of dress. But I mention this to call attention to the fact that while the uniform he wore may have been nearly threadbare, clean but sometimes nearly worn out, it was a distinctive sign of his austerity. Austerity not only for himself but also for his family, for his children, for all who were around him—austerity he taught by example.

A<small>ND WITH THAT</small>, comrades, I've reached the end of my remarks. When he said good-bye, Che told me: "Yes, it's possible to win a war in this way." And he added: "We will win."

Che died in near absolute solitude, conscious of not having won that war, because it's evident from his diary that he knew he was surrounded. I mourned his death a great deal, as well as the fact he had not won that war. Three days later, when I flew to Rome, I found the city nearly covered with portraits of Che. It was a surprise to arrive in Rome and find the city filled with images of the Heroic Guerrilla. Written everywhere were the words "Che lives!" And then I realized that Che had won that war. Because wars are won not only with military victories. Wars are also won with victories such as setting a moral example for many people.

That is the war Che must win among us. That is the war I call us to, so that in this twentieth anniversary we will always have Che present, in order to win under the leadership of Fidel.

Thank you.

The Communist Manifesto

by Karl Marx and Frederick Engels

The founding program of the revolutionary working-class movement. 48 pp., $3.95

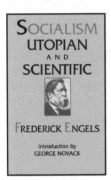

Socialism: Utopian and Scientific

by Frederick Engels

Explains the origins of the materialist world outlook of the modern communist workers' movement. 63 pp., $3.00

Marx and Engels on the United States

Articles and correspondence on the Civil War and other key questions in the U.S. class struggle from the 1840s to 1890s. 391 pp., $15.95

Imperialism: The Highest Stage of Capitalism

by V.I. Lenin

Outlines the nature of imperialism and the imperialist epoch — the twentieth century. $3.95

Challenge of the Left Opposition

by Leon Trotsky

Documents the fight of the communist opposition in the 1920s against the reactionary political and economic policies of the rising bureaucratic caste in the Soviet Union led by Stalin. Three volumes, vols. 1 and 3, $27.95 each, vol. 2, $30.95

The Revolution Betrayed

What Is the Soviet Union and Where Is It Going?

by Leon Trotsky

Classic study of the bureaucratic degeneration of the Soviet Union under Stalin. Explains the roots of the social and political crisis shaking the former Soviet bloc countries in the 1990s. 314 pp., $19.95

For a Workers' and Farmers' Government in the United States

by Jack Barnes

Strategic questions facing working people in the transition from capitalism to socialism. 61 pp., 8½-by-11 format, $7.00

SEE PAGE 2 FOR DISTRIBUTORS

THE CREATIVITY OF CHE'S
ECONOMIC THOUGHT

by Carlos Tablada

A S PART OF THE rectification process, Fidel has proposed a thorough study of Ernesto Che Guevara's writings on building socialism and communism. Che's thought constitutes a rich source of ideas and solutions, of socialist formulas for constructing the new society.

This body of ideas, which Che applied and tested in practice, is still not widely known, but it is important to the entire world.

When we read Che, we feel the timeliness of his ideas. There is nothing unusual about this. Che, like his teacher Fidel, was a visionary. He was capable of seeing beyond the immediate, of keeping both the forest and the trees in sight. As is evident today, Fidel and Che foresaw many things that were later confirmed by the course of history.

Humanity needs fresh ideas, new points of view. We can draw sustenance from Che's writings because they probe deeply into the nature of humanity's problems.

Every socialist country faces the dual problem of establishing an efficient system of economic administration and management while at the same time creating new human values free of individualism and selfishness. That is, they all face the task of developing the communist education of working people as an essential part of creating and extending socialist society.

The international context has changed in the last twenty

This article first appeared in the May-June 1989 issue of Cuba Socialista. *It has been revised by the author for publication here. Carlos Tablada is an economist who teaches at the University of Havana and has worked in the management of Cuban state enterprises. The translation is copyright © 1991 by Pathfinder Press and is reprinted by permission.*

years. But in terms of the concrete historical, social, and economic problems faced by Asia, Africa, Latin America, and even the developed countries, the situation is essentially the same as the one Che confronted.

If there is a real difference, it is that the contradictions and conflicts have deepened. Poverty, exploitation, homelessness, and inequality have increased. The foreign debt has jumped a hundredfold. The world we live in has become more explosive.

At the same time, over the last twenty years millions of people in Latin America, Africa, and Asia have gained a deeper political consciousness and a better understanding of how their societies and economies function.

In the developed capitalist countries, a growing number of people understand that the gains of science and technology and the living standards of societies with enormous resources cannot continue to coexist with a world situation in which a majority of humanity is exploited and oppressed.

Che's contributions cannot be dismembered

In our country, doubts and one-sided interpretations of Che's economic thought have sometimes been raised. For example, some people recognize *only* that Che excelled in the application of Marxism-Leninism. The same individuals often contend that the budgetary finance system created by Che was suited solely to the concrete needs of the first stage of the revolution.

Accepting these two premises tends to make it impossible to use from Che anything other than a few isolated ideas—ideas that do not lie at the center of his thought. Some aspects, some methods of his work can be adopted, it is felt, including his rigorous standards, his emphasis on financial controls (accounting, cost analysis, auditing), and the priority he gave to organization. It is also acknowledged that Che had the scientific merit of applying the general principles of Marxism-Leninism to a particular situation—the building of socialism in Cuba during the first years of the revolution.

But this also usually means asserting that the efficiency of the budgetary finance system could not be verified in practice; and contending that the system suffered from an extreme centralization in economic decision-making.

To fully grasp the value of Che's thought for building socialism and communism, we need to go into the matter more deeply.

We Cubans should be the first to study, explain, and systematize Che's contributions to the theory and practice of Marxism and Leninism. And as Fidel has pointed out, the rectification process itself requires taking up this task. It is the fundamental starting point for fully resolving our problems.

FROM THE EARLY 1960s on, Fidel Castro and Che Guevara stressed the need for a critical and analytical approach in building socialism. They pointed to the dangers involved in trodding the beaten paths of capitalism. Life has proven them correct. Che devoted himself to deepening his study of theory and making it an instrument for the practical work of building a new society.

Twenty-five years ago Che, along with Fidel, recognized the stagnation, schematism, and dogmatism into which an important current of revolutionary thought had fallen. Both Che and Fidel should be seen as precursors of a new approach in Marxist social science. In particular, they represent a new approach to the political economy of socialism, to the theory and practice of building socialism and communism.[1]

In his speech commemorating labor's international holiday on May 1, 1966, Fidel Castro pointed out:

> It could be said that while industrial technology and science in general have developed in an incredible fashion, the social sciences remain underdeveloped. We have heard formulas, we have read the textbooks, but nothing teaches as well as a revolution. At the same time as one must learn how to properly assess and evaluate the experiences of other peoples, each people has to make an effort not to copy but to make a contribution to those underdeveloped sciences of politics and society.
>
> We are going to develop our ideas. We understand that Marxist-Leninist ideas require constant development. We

ENDNOTES FOR THIS ARTICLE BEGIN ON PAGE 186.

are aware that a certain stagnation has occurred in this field. We even see acceptance, almost universal acceptance, of formulas that in our opinion can lead away from the essence of Marxism-Leninism.[2]

There is a high degree of identity and similarity between the ideas of Che and Fidel. They held the same principles, fought for the same objectives, and shared the same belief in the possibility of transforming human beings.

For example, their conception of economic development is practically identical. In 1979, Fidel summed it up as follows: "Development primarily involves attention to human beings, who should be the protagonists and the goal of all development efforts."[3]

Che did not view economic development as an end in itself. Development of a society has meaning only if it serves to transform men and women, enhance their creative capacities, and draw them beyond self-centeredness. The transition to the kingdom of freedom is a voyage from "me" to "us." And socialism cannot carry out this transition with what Che called "the dull instruments left to us by capitalism."[4] We cannot advance toward communism if life under socialism is organized like a competition among wolves, as in the previous society.

Socialism is not a finished, perfect system in which all the details have been ironed out and where all the answers are known. Our system has flaws, shortcomings, and aspects requiring further development. Within the framework of socialist principles, Che Guevara sought solutions to the concrete problems of establishing a socialist system in Cuba. And within that framework he also tried to correct the flaws he found in theoretical writings on the period of transition to socialism.

It is obvious that in 1989 it would make no sense to try to mechanically apply, in exactly the same way, each formula or solution Che proposed and put into practice more than twenty years ago. Che himself would not have done that; it was never his way of thinking. Cuban society and the international context have changed during the intervening period. But I do believe that the system of managing the economy that arises out of the rectification process—whatever name it may be given—will stem not from the economic accounting system but rather from the thought of Che and Fidel.

Any evaluation we make should be based on a series of factors. First, a full, unprejudiced, and objective assessment of the experience of building socialism in Cuba over the last thirty years. Second, an assessment of the experiences of building socialism in other parts of the world. And last but not least, communist ideals and Marxist-Leninist theory on the new society.

Che's study of Marxism

Within Cuba and abroad there are people who think that Che began his study of Marxist economic theory in 1959. They believe his work in this field began following his appointment to economic posts (head of INRA's Industry Department, president of the National Bank of Cuba, and minister of industry)[5] and, more concretely, following the arrival of the Hispanic-Soviet academic Anastasio Mansilla, professor of political economy.

Such a view does not correspond with the facts. When he was sixteen years old, Ernesto began to read Karl Marx, Frederick Engels, and V.I. Lenin. Among other works, he became familiar with *Capital* by Marx and the *Manifesto of the Communist Party* by Marx and Engels. At this age he began to draw up a philosophical dictionary. During the years of his university studies, he studied other works, such as *Anti-Dühring* by Engels and *Imperialism: The Highest Stage of Capitalism* and *The State and Revolution* by Lenin.

In his travels through Latin America and the Caribbean prior to 1959, Che did more than simply employ his medical knowledge and conduct research on allergies. He devoted himself principally to studying the history and culture of the countries he visited, scouring their museums and ruins. He had a passion for archaeology, indigenous cultures, and the most advanced social ideas.

Che's knowledge of the reality of the Americas led him to deepen his study of Marxism-Leninism. Both his correspondence with family members and his written works from this period (1954-56) show the degree to which he devoted himself to systematic study, in particular to political economy, statistics, and related fields. Some examples:

> One may ask: Why does the United States—a very highly industrialized country with all the characteristics of a capitalist empire—not feel the contradictions that pit capital and labor against each other in all-out struggle? The response must be sought in the special conditions of this country to the north. With the exception of the Blacks—who are segregated and are the embryo of the first serious rebellion—the other workers (those with jobs, naturally) enjoy enormous wages in comparison to what capitalist enterprises usually give. The reason for this is that the difference between what is normally required by the needs of surplus value and what is currently paid is more than compensated for by groups of workers from two great communities of nations: Asians and Latin Americans.[6]
>
> Havana in particular beckons me; I want to fill my heart with the countryside, well mixed with passages from Lenin.[7]
>
> I am strong and optimistic, frequently climb the volcanos, visit the ruins, and read a great deal of St. Karl and his disciples.[8]
>
> In reality I have little to tell of my own life, since I spend my time exercising and reading. I believe I'll end up a powerhouse in economic questions, although I may have forgotten how to take a pulse and listen through a stethoscope (which I never did very well anyway). My path seems to diverge gradually and firmly from clinical medicine, but never so far as to lose my nostalgia for the hospital. What I told you about a professorship in physiology was a lie, but not much of one. It was a lie because I never really thought I would accept the appointment; but the proposal was made and there was a high degree of probability that they would grant me the post, given my interview and everything else. In any event, this now belongs to the past. St. Karl has won a studious adherent.[9]
>
> Of course, all scientific work has gone by the boards and now I am solely a relentless reader of Karl, Fred, and

the boys. I forgot to tell you that when I was arrested they found a number of pamphlets in Russian, in addition to a letter from the Mexican-Russian Exchange Institute where, out of conditioned reflexes, I was studying the language.[10]

As for myself, I'm in the process of changing the direction of my studies. In the past, for better or worse, I concentrated on medicine while devoting my free time to an informal study of St. Karl. The new stage of my life demands a change in the direction of my studies as well. St. Karl now comes first. He is the axis of my studies and will remain so for the years that remain to me in the outermost layer of this spheroid. . . .

In addition, I was beginning to draw a series of conclusions that clashed sharply with my trajectory as fundamentally an adventurer. I decided to tackle first things first, to enter into battle against the way things are, a shield upon my arm, like a character in a fantasy; and then, if the windmills didn't crack my skull, to write.[11]

O̶N THE EVE of his departure aboard the *Granma,* Ernesto was hiding out at the house of Dr. Alfonso Bauer, a Guatemalan. In 1977 Bauer gave an interview in which he commented, among other things, on the state of the room Guevara occupied.

His room was a complete pandemonium—an unmade bed, a maté drinking straw here, a small cooking stove there, articles of clothing scattered about, and a half dozen books lying open as though they were all being read at the same time. Among them were *State and Revolution* by Lenin, *Capital* by Marx, a textbook on battlefield surgery, and a book of mine, *Cómo opera el capital yanqui en Centro América* [How U.S. capital operates in Central America].[12]

In my opinion, the fundamental aspects of Che's ideas and practice remain applicable today. Adjustments should be made to take account of changes that have occurred since then. But this must be done *without altering his fundamental starting point,* without altering his critical approach toward certain conceptions of how to build socialism during the transition to communist society.

Beginning from an understanding that "communism is a phenomenon of consciousness and not solely a phenomenon of production,"[13] Che devoted himself to the task of creating a system of economic management that, while maintaining this focus, would draw upon

• advanced accounting techniques that permitted more effective controls and an efficient centralized management; also, studies and practical application of the methods of centralization and decentralization used by the capitalist monopolies;

• computer techniques applied to the economy and to management, and the application of mathematical methods to the economy;

• techniques of programming and supervising production;

• budgetary techniques as instruments of planning and supervision through finances;

• administrative techniques of implementing economic controls;

• participation by the masses in the management of the economy, direct motivation of the worker, and workers' identification with the final product; and

• the practical and theoretical experiences of the socialist countries.

FOR CHE, building socialism and communism is a phenomenon of production, organization, and consciousness. It is not simply an administrative, technical, and economic task. Rather it is a task demanding an ideological, technical, political, and economic approach. Che underscored the importance of *integrating* all these elements, which he brought together in his conception of the economic management system needed to build socialism, that is, the budgetary finance system. Che insisted that the fundamental element is the development of consciousness, with the final objective being the new human being. Simultaneous with creating the new material and technical foundations for socialism, it is necessary to develop a system of education that assures the creation of consciousness and, consequently, the formation of the new man and woman.

With the budgetary finance system, Che sought to organize the economy and attain maximum efficiency in economic management; to deepen and develop the consciousness of the masses; and to unify and develop the world socialist system. He developed the various aspects of the system in both theory and practice, unifying them in a harmonious and logical whole. He called on the party and the youth organization to serve as the active material force in carrying out an extensive effort of political education.

Few people are aware that the budgetary finance system worked with a high degree of efficiency during the opening years of the revolution despite the circumstances then prevailing nationally and in the Ministry of Industry. At the time, the ministry directed 70 percent of the country's industrial production (sugar, light industry, basic industry, a sector of the food industry, machine tools, construction materials, pharmaceuticals, and others). It had responsibility for some 260,000 workers, 48 consolidated enterprises, and about 1,500 establishments. In all, it administered basic means of production valued at 1.5 billion pesos, of which 930 million were of capitalist origin.[14]

The budgetary finance system worked despite enormous obstacles. These included the U.S. blockade; the loss of experts and trained administrative personnel through emigration to the United States; a shortage of technicians and trained personnel of all types (for example, the Ministry of Industry and all its departments never had more than 473 engineers at one time);[15] difficulties caused by shortages of spare parts, raw materials, and equipment; one million people only recently literate; a work force with low levels of skill; lack of discipline among workers; and reliance on administrators who often had no more than a second-grade education.

Do Cuban enterprises today match the level of organization, controls, management, efficiency, and systematization they had in the consolidated enterprises under Che in December 1964? From my personal experience, I believe the answer is no. We have not matched them in terms of financial discipline in billing and payment; inventory control; accuracy and truthfulness in primary data; or cost analysis at the level of the production unit.

It has been suggested that we adopt some of the subsystems that made up the budgetary finance system, disengaging them and grafting them onto the economic accounting system. But the budgetary finance system is a coherent whole; it has an internal structure based on theoretical and practical premises that have been fully substantiated.

This point is important. We should not lose sight of the fact that this is a budgetary finance *system*. Indeed, its character as a system is one of its most vital features: it is what makes possible the system's continuing enrichment and innovation. Che drew up the budgetary finance system because he did not agree with the economic accounting system.

The budgetary finance system *has no antecedents*. It should not be confused, simply because of its name, with budgetary systems that have been utilized previously in sister socialist countries and, later on, in our country. In its fundamental principles and methods, the budgetary finance system is unique.

Economic planning and political consciousness

I want to take a little time to discuss the relationship between Che's general conception of the political economy of socialism, his theoretical views on the period of the transition to socialism, and his views on the different systems of economic management. I do this because it is one of the things most likely to be confused; it has been subjected to the most varying interpretations. Some compañeros say there is no such relationship. Others say that if one exists, it is not essential. This reflects a failure to fully grasp the creativity and scope of Che's outstanding contribution.

In the book *Che Guevara: Economics and Politics in the Transition to Socialism*, I pointed out that it was necessary to differentiate between technical and political aspects of managing the economy.

Che argued that technical procedures could be taken from wherever they were the most developed. The new society could adapt them to its needs without fear of *contagion* by bourgeois ideology, *so long as the process was limited* to the adoption or assimilation of technical norms of managing and instituting controls over production.

From the point of view of ideology, however, Che held that the new society should not develop or rely on the economic mechanisms, incentives, and management criteria that pertain to the capitalist mode of production.

In other words, Che called for critical assimilation of the most advanced techniques in economic management and in establishing controls over production. But in terms of motivating the producers, he rejected using and developing the dull instruments left to us by capitalism.

Even in its first moments, the period of transition to socialism and communism does not have to have its character determined by the law of value and the other market-economy categories implied by the operation of this law. The law of value's operation during the transition to socialism should be approached as simply one of the limitations we have inherited from capitalism.

Che believed that political economy in the Soviet Union and the Eastern European countries had not fully grasped and developed what was new in socialist and communist society. He called for giving more thought to the fundamental laws of economics, stressing the moral and political factor. He felt that economic planning should be viewed as humanity's first chance to harness economic forces.

CHE DEVELOPED the thought of Marx, Engels, and Lenin. He linked economic planning to the concepts of anticapitalist revolution and the dictatorship of the proletariat. In this context, economic planning marks the emergence of a new way of making history. For the first time in history, humanity has taken on the role of consciously transforming society.

Economic planning is the *only* instrument that makes it possible to develop the productive forces, form new human relations, create the new human being, and reach the stage of communist society. Such steps are possible only if and when the economic plan is drawn up and implemented according to certain premises. In other words, planning is not a magic wand for solving problems. The plan is created by human beings and is part of a general conception. In Che's view, the economic plan is neither a fetish nor a straitjacket. It is a basic tool for building socialist society.

Thus, to reduce the concept of planning to merely its economic components, Che thought, would be to deform it from the outset and limit its possibilities. In Che's opinion, the plan embraced *material relations as a whole* (in the sense Marx gave to the term). For that reason the economic plan should incorporate and unite two elements:

1. Creating the foundation for economic development of the new society, as well as for economic regulation and controls.

2. Creating a new type of human relations, a new human being.

This raises a principle of planning, and thus a principle of the period of transition to communism that cannot be overlooked without distorting the plan and endangering the transition to communism itself. This is the principle that the effectiveness of the plan cannot be evaluated *solely* by whether or not it improves economic management and, therefore, augments the goods available to society. Nor can it be evaluated by the income obtained in the production process.

The real measure of the plan's effectiveness lies in its potential to improve economic management in terms of advancing toward the central objective: communist society. In other words, the true gauge lies in the plan's ability to combine what is rational socially with what is rational economically. Its effectiveness can be measured by the degree to which the economic apparatus helps create the technical and material base for the new society and, *at the same time,* spurs a transformation in the habits and values of those who participate in the productive process, thereby helping to create and instill the new communist values.

Raúl Castro explained it this way:

> Let us set aside theoretical discussion and unjustified criticisms. In the fifteen years since 1953, and in worse conditions than today, we have grown accustomed to hearing such criticisms. It is deeds and our people that will have the final say! ·
>
> We do not deny the difficulty of the road we have

taken. It is especially difficult when we have to break with prefabricated schemas, rigid dogmas, and established myths, and at the same time continue fighting firmly against the many shortcomings we still have.

When a people becomes conscious of what it is capable of, it displays a sweeping, contagious, and revolutionary passion. . . .

A spirit of work creates a spirit of work; consciousness engenders consciousness; courage and faith engender courage and faith; an honest attitude engenders more honest attitudes; love of all society, of the entire people, and of all humankind engenders more love among men.

But if we teach selfishness and money, it will engender more selfishness. Personal ambition will engender more personal ambition. Opportunism will engender more opportunism. Corruption will engender more corruption. Ferocious individualism will engender more individualism.

That is why we refuse to erect an altar to the god of "money" and prostrate the consciousness of men at its feet![16]

CHE DISCOVERED that virtually the entire body of literature on the political economy of the period of the transition to socialism lacked original conceptual tools suited to the topic. From the theoretical point of view, this body of literature tends to distort the very object of study by applying Marxist categories that pertain to the analysis of capitalism. In doing so, theory loses the possibility of critically examining the new reality.

Che noted that the actual meaning of the words *economic accounting system* had always been obscure. In fact, its meaning appears to have changed over the years. It must be understood that this form of administrative management is not an economic category that is absolutely necessary and obligatory. The economic accounting system is simply a series of measures for implementing controls in, managing, and running socialized enterprises. It emerged with its particular features in a number of socialist countries during a given historical period.

Che warned that we must take care not to utilize practice as the sole yardstick, while entirely ignoring theoretical abstraction. He also warned against indiscriminate use of apologetics.

> Unfortunately, in the eyes of most of our people, and in mine as well, apologetics for a system can have more impact than scientific analysis of it.[17]

Owing to the very way it functions, the economic accounting system is inseparably linked to the dull instruments left to us by capitalism. It cannot work without capitalist economic mechanisms and categories borrowed from the capitalist market system. It assimilates them not as limitations to socialism, but as virtues added to it.

If we utilize these categories—as well as the economic and social structures and relations they describe in capitalist society—it will be difficult to deal with a reality whose characteristics are not understood theoretically.

The law of value is an element of Marxist economic theory that has been torn out of its context as the fundamental law of motion of *capitalism* and converted into a fundamental pillar of more than one theory on the political economy of the period of the transition to *socialism*. Che's critical analysis of such use of the law of value is one of his greatest contributions to Marxist-Leninist theory.

Che's position on using the law of value and other capitalist categories to direct the economy during the transition period, as well as on their role in formulating a theory of building communist society, can be summed up as follows:

1. He rejected the law of value as the guiding principle in the period of transition to communism.

2. He made the following distinction: It is one thing to *acknowledge the existence* of a series of capitalist relations that necessarily persist during the transition period (including the law of value, given its character as an economic law—that is, as an expression of certain economic tendencies). It is quite another to affirm the possibility of managing the economy by the *conscious and fundamental use* of the law of value and its corollaries.

3. He rejected the view that the period of transition to com-

munism—even in its first phases—has to unfold in accordance with the law of value and the other categories of commodity production implied by its use.

4. He rejected the view that not only recommends use of the law of value and monetary-commodity relations in the transition period, but also asserts the need to *develop* these relations—which reach their highest development under capitalism—as a vehicle for achieving communist society.

5. He rejected the idea that it was impossible to avoid using "the *commodity* category in relations among state enterprises." Instead, he considered "all such establishments to be part of the single large enterprise that is the state."[18]

6. He held it necessary to implement economic policies that lead to the gradual withering away of the old relations, including the market, money (so long as its functions are distorted), and thus the lever of direct material self-interest. Or, more accurately, he believed it was necessary to implement policies that lead to the gradual elimination of the conditions that give rise to these relations.

In this regard, Che explained:

> We understand that capitalist categories are retained for a time and that the length of this time cannot be determined beforehand. But the characteristics of the transition period are those of a society throwing off its old bonds in order to arrive quickly at the new stage.
>
> The *tendency* must be, in our opinion, to eliminate as vigorously as possible the old categories, including the market, money, and, therefore, the lever of material interest—or, to put it better, to eliminate the conditions for their existence. Otherwise, one would have to assume that the task of building socialism in a backward society is something in the nature of a historical accident and that its leaders, in order to make up for the "mistake," should set about consolidating all the categories inherent in the intermediate society. All that would remain as foundations of the new society would be the distribution of income according to work and the tendency toward elimination of man's exploitation of man.
>
> These things by themselves seem inadequate to bring

about the gigantic change in consciousness necessary to tackle the transition. That change must take place through the multifaceted action of all the new relations, through education and socialist morality—with the individualistic way of thinking that direct material incentives instill in consciousness acting as a brake on the development of man as a social being.[19]

7. He rejected the practice of indiscriminately using capitalist categories. If capitalist categories such as "the commodity as the economic cell, profitability, individual material interest as a lever, etc.,"[20] are used in building the new society, they will rapidly take on an existence of their own, in the end imposing their own influence on relations among men.

8. He explained the consequences of giving free reign to the law of value in the period of transition to communism. Not only does it imply the impossibility of fundamentally restructuring social relations, since it means perpetuating the "umbilical cord" that ties alienated man to society. But it also leads toward a hybrid system in which a fundamental transformation of the social nature of man and society will not occur.

9. According to Che, "In our view communism is a phenomenon of consciousness and not solely a phenomenon of production. We cannot arrive at communism through the simple mechanical accumulation of quantities of goods made available to the people. By doing that we would get somewhere, to be sure, to some peculiar form of socialism. But what Marx defined as communism, what is aspired to in general as communism, cannot be attained if man is not conscious. That is, if he does not have a new consciousness toward society."[21]

Che believed that the law of value operates to a certain extent in a country building socialism, given the holdovers from capitalist society based on generalized commodity production and exchange. The budgetary finance system recognized the law of value, monetary-commodity relations, and the commodity as such, but only in relations between the state, cooperatives, and individuals and, on an international level, in foreign trade. It did not utilize monetary-commodity relations within the state sector and rejected the use of commodity relations between state enterprises.

In the transition period new socialist relations should be developed, not monetary-commodity relations. The law of value should be eliminated, not by decree but through a process of gradual withering away as we develop the new forms inherent in the system we are building.

$\mathbf{A}$s the means of production are transferred to the revolutionary state, new relations of production emerge and become established. This stage requires *a new conception* of production, of its inner workings and its goals. It also requires new *ways* of operating the mechanisms of supervision, organization, management, and incentives.

Marx and Engels noted in this regard:

> In all previous revolutions the mode of activity always remained unchanged and it was only a question of a different distribution of this activity, a new distribution of labour to other persons, whilst the communist revolution is directed against the hitherto existing *mode* of activity.[22]

During this stage in the transition to socialism, some means of production remain in the hands of capitalists and small producers, both private and cooperative. Even in the period when commodity production still exists for a sector of production, however, measures taken by the revolutionary state on social questions as well as on strictly economic ones tend to substantially modify the way the law of value functions.

These measures include, among others: lowering the rent on housing; providing medical care and social assistance either free of charge or at "below-market prices"; setting and controlling prices to combat counterrevolutionary speculation; establishing control over foreign currency, foreign trade, and domestic wholesale trade; bringing previously marginalized sectors of the population into the economic life of the country; and taking steps to eliminate unemployment.

In practice, such measures make it impossible for the law of value to reign.

The law of value no longer establishes the quantities in which commodities are produced or exchanged. It no longer determines how labor power is allotted among different sectors of the economy, or how resources are allocated. It ceases being a regulatory mechanism. Of key importance in this regard is the fact that prices are no longer set spontaneously, through market fluctuations in supply and demand, with all the consequences this implies. These market operations are responsible for the automatic, anarchic, and brutal way in which proportions and equilibrium are established in capitalist society.

In this stage of the revolution the leadership establishes distribution not on the basis of value, but in accordance with its political program; the concrete conditions of the country and the rest of the world; and the revolution's political, ideological, and military strength.

What is important in the management of society's productive forces is the overall data of economic and social costs and benefits. What does this mean? That on the basis of an exact and rigorous analysis of the costs of production and the value of the goods produced, socialism can rationally set prices above or below the value of a particular item. In other words, prices of particular items become interchangeable so long as required levels of "profitability" (understood as overall equilibrium in the management of society's productive resources—meaning nothing more than the existence of a surplus product) and efficiency are maintained overall, and so long as the sum total of the prices tends to coincide with the value created.

This might be taken as proof that in the final analysis the law of value does govern under socialism, that it regulates the overall economic and social equilibrium. That would be a pure illusion, however. Ensuring the necessary social surplus product is a feature inherent in any society if it is to continue to exist. But this elementary principle, this measure of economic rationality, *is not* the law of value. The law of value is simply the theory that explains *the manner* in which this equilibrium is established—spontaneously—in bourgeois society. The plan, for its part, is *the manner* in which this equilibrium is attained—consciously and rationally—in socialist and communist societies.

On the other hand, the function and advantages of the plan in comparison with capitalism do not rest in establishing the costs of manufacturing a given product in order to set its price. The plan has a different task: to serve as a tool in rationally and consciously building the new society. Its main advantage is precisely that the plan, unlike the capitalist business executive, is not bound by the level of profitability of a particular production unit, or even an entire sector of production. Everything it manages can be financed centrally and regulated on the basis of overall proportions. The key to its success is the rigor, detail, precision, and accuracy of both the data at its disposal and the analysis of that data. The aim is to establish the proportions that assure the successful reproduction of the relations of socialist production.

Che saw cost analysis as the fundamental way of measuring the efficiency of establishments and enterprises. He pointed to its usefulness as a method of supervision and management. He viewed it as the ideal way to optimize the expenditure of social labor. This would make it possible to reduce the amount of such labor per unit produced and thereby increase—*in real terms*—the productivity and efficiency of establishments, enterprises, branches of industry, and society as a whole.

THE FOREGOING is essential for understanding the new ideas put forward by Che and the Cuban revolution in this domain. It is not that Che wanted to skip stages and rush things. And he had no illusion that an accelerated development of consciousness could impose a pace faster than what history made possible.

We should not forget that today—almost thirty-six years after the attack on the Moncada garrison[23] and thirty years after the triumph of the revolution—there are some who still do not understand the essence of our revolution because they are prisoners of dogmas and schemas. Our revolution has been, ever since Moncada, a "revolt against oligarchies and against revolutionary dogmas."[24]

Che said that we had to *concern ourselves* right from the *beginning* with the creation of a *new* consciousness and a *new* morality. He said that this had to occur simultaneously with efforts to develop the material and technical foundations of the new society.

Che understood that the new consciousness would result from a gradual process of transforming the social structures, that it would inevitably emerge from this process. He understood that the possibilities for transforming man were therefore determined more by the transformation of the social relations of production, and by the correct selection of the motivating levers, than by appeals to consciousness.

I N "Socialism and Man in Cuba," Che sums up brilliantly the factors responsible for the shortcomings in revolutionary theory and particularly of socialist political economy—some of which we have pointed out.

> If we add to this the scholasticism that has held back the development of Marxist philosophy and impeded a systematic treatment of the transition period, whose political economy has not been developed, we must agree that we are still in diapers and that it is necessary to devote ourselves to investigating all the principal characteristics of this period before elaborating an economic and political theory of greater scope.
>
> The resulting theory will, no doubt, put great stress on the two pillars of the construction of socialism: the education of the new man and the development of technology.[25]

"The law of value and the plan are two terms linked by a contradiction and its resolution," Che pointed out. They play a contradictory role; they are headed in two different directions.

> We can therefore state that centralized planning is the mode of existence of socialist society, its defining characteristic, and the point at which man's consciousness finally succeeds in synthesizing and directing the economy toward its goal: the full liberation of the human being within the framework of communist society.[26]

Every mode of production has to calculate how much social labor is expended. In socialist and communist society such calculations are and will become more precise, more conscious, and less spontaneous. At the same time, they will less and less be drawn from market analyses. In these societies, the calculation of social labor does not have to be linked to the development of monetary-commodity relations.[27]

In a society based on the production of commodities, production, distribution, and the reproduction of congealed social labor are determined *after the fact*. In socialist society, however, these elements can be determined *at the outset* through economic planning.

The problem lies in the ideological influence that commodity fetishism continues to exert over the consciousness of the individual. During the transition to socialism, people continue to believe they are seeing the law of value, commodities, and monetary-commodity relations, when in reality they are witnessing their opposites.

> We believe that the inconsistency among the defenders of the economic accounting system stems from the fact that they follow Marxist analysis to a certain point but then, in order to continue their line of argument, they have to take a leap (leaving the "missing link" in the middle). Concretely, the defenders of the economic accounting system have never correctly explained how the concept of the commodity, in its essence, can be applied to transactions [among enterprises and institutions] in the state sector. Nor have they explained how the law of value can be used "intelligently" in the socialist sector, with its distorted markets.[28]

Profit vs. social needs: contradiction of economic accounting system

I believe that the economic accounting system tends to foster a certain fetishism. The category of profit tends to cover over and divert attention from the essential point: production—producing the variety of goods required to meet social needs. The economic accounting system measures production efficiency by profit and profitability. But these are categories that in essence pertain to the market, that attain their fullest development under capitalism. And in the process of developing, they tend to impede the creation of use-values that are essential to the satisfaction of needs. That is, they tend to impede the central aim of socialism.

Marx explained what happens in bourgeois, capitalist societies based on commodity production. Private ownership determines that the only way isolated producers have to relate to one another is through the market. The varying quantities of labor to be expended are thus regulated after the fact, in an anarchic and spontaneous way. Value itself serves as the fundamental criterion, as the essential element in the process of expending labor.

Marx pointed out in this regard:

> All commodities are *non–use-values for their owners, and use-values for their non-owners.* Consequently, they must all change hands. But this changing of hands constitutes their exchange, and their exchange puts them in relation with each other as values and realizes them as values. Hence commodities must be realized as values before they can be realized as use-values.
>
> On the other hand, *they must stand the test as use-values before they can be realized as values.* For the labour expended on them only counts in so far as it is expended in a form which is useful for others. However, only the act of exchange can prove whether their labour is useful for others, and its product consequently capable of satisfying the needs of others.[29]

IN SOCIALIST SOCIETY, however, the means of production are socially owned. Use-values, the practical features of commodities, and the quantity and quality of a product become the fundamental elements of exchange. From the outset, economic planning permits regulation of the various activities that the producers should maintain among themselves. For the first time, there is a *direct* relationship between consumer needs and what is produced.

In capitalist society, this relationship is indirect and bears the hallmarks of fetishism. Relations between human beings take on the appearance of relations between things. The real aim of production becomes the commodity's brief moment in the marketplace. The commodity, an inert object, becomes the regulator of activity among human beings.

In socialist society, on the other hand, there is a direct relationship between human needs and the form in which those needs are satisfied. This relationship is concretized prior to the initiation of the process of production, in a planned and conscious way. The commodity no longer comes first, ahead of the human being. Work is directly social. The producer's main attention is focused on the useful, practical, and tangible aspects of work, on its qualitative and quantitative character (which includes economizing in the expenditure of social labor). Value appears directly as a social relationship of production, consciously established.

Recent experiences in both Cuba and other countries that use the economic accounting system make one thing clear. There is a definite tendency under this system for the production of use-values to become a secondary priority, despite its fundamental importance in the transition to socialism. This exercise in fetishism in turn gives rise to additional monetary-commodity relations. The economic stagnation and exhaustion that accompany the use of the economic accounting system demand—in return for continuing to develop the economy—new and deeper monetary-commodity relations. That is, they demand new steps backward.

Historically, the process of exchange has in practice increasingly departed from the law of value. It is only in less-developed commodity-producing societies that this law operates in a pure form.[30]

In my view, fetishism gains ground in man's consciousness when there is a failure to recognize that, of three elements basic to the existence and development of commodity relations, two have disappeared or tend to disappear or diminish during the transition period. These two elements are private ownership of the means of production (which is fundamental) and relative economic isolation. The latter tends to gradually decline as society becomes more *integrated*. From the outset social ownership of the means of production gradually imbues work with a directly social character. The tendency is therefore to *reduce* the social and economic differences among producers, not to deepen them.

We are masters of the means of production and of our destiny. But the fetishism created by the economic accounting system does not reduce human alienation, nor does it make individuals feel a part of this process. In fact, far from progressively eliminating alienation, it actually increases it to the extent that it promotes creating and obtaining values (money) as opposed to use-values, which alone are capable of really satisfying human needs.

The fetishism inherent in the economic accounting system stems from the fetishism of monetary-commodity relations. Indeed, it promotes an extension and reinforcement of these relations.

What Che sought to accomplish was to join together—in one living and unified body of theory—economic production, on the one hand, and, on the other, the production and reproduction of the mode of activity in which economic production occurs. That is, he sought to include in his theory the social relations that individuals establish both within and outside the process of production. In other words, he believed there were concerns above and beyond simply producing more. It was also necessary to ask: What is being produced? How? Why? For whom? And for what ends?

We must produce material goods. But at the same time, we also have to produce the person who is going to run the machinery, who is going to keep track of, oversee, administer, supervise, and direct the process of production.

CHE UNDERSTOOD the consequences of establishing capitalist, commodity-based, or pseudocapitalist mechanisms. He understood that if people live, work, and act under the effects of these mechanisms, no amount of political work can transform them into models of virtue, of the new morality. If the mechanisms compel you to act as a capitalist administrator, a "market fanatic," or a "two-bit businessman," or as a worker motivated by direct material self-interest, through the use of money—then you cannot think or act as a worker motivated by the interests of society as a whole. You cannot become a better or finer human being. Social being determines social consciousness. Or as Raúl put it, selfishness, the goal of obtaining nothing but money, only engenders more selfishness; ferocious individualism only engenders more individualism.

The quantity and quality of the material goods produced is

not the only thing that is important. Also important is the *manner* in which they are produced, the social relations that flow from the mode of production and distribution of the product.

Che saw consciousness as an active element, a material force, an engine to develop the material and technical foundations. This in no way signifies, however, that he allowed himself to become immersed in romantic and unrealizable dreams. He was fully aware of the nature of human beings as they climbed out of the muck of bourgeois society:

> The problem is that people are not perfect, far from it. We have to improve systems of controls to detect the very first infraction, because the first one leads to all the others. People might be very good the first time. But when, through indiscipline, they commit the error of taking something for personal use, intending to replace it in two or three days, this can then spread to the point of their becoming thieves, becoming traitors, falling increasingly into crime.[31]

That is why he designed a system—the budgetary finance system—that took existing limitations into account but also *promoted* a new attitude toward work. Che was convinced that consciousness would engender consciousness, that virtue and faithfulness would engender virtue and faithfulness, that honesty would engender more honesty, that a good example would multiply good examples.[32]

Che took up a theme that was incomprehensible to many of his contemporaries, and that remains so to some people today. That is the relationship between base and superstructure, between social being and social consciousness under socialism, between the modification of the conditions of life and the modification of human activity, between the production of life and the production of consciousness.

Che was convinced that advances, stagnation, and regressions in the ideological plane could not be explained simplistically. That is, he did not believe that they were merely a reflection of the quality of the political work or ideological education that had been carried out. Because that political work itself, he held, had in turn been conditioned by the totality of material relations referred to above.

To be aware of and take part in the conscious creation of a
new society is quite different from skipping over stages or imposing a more rapid pace of developing consciousness. The
initial triumph of the revolution opens up the possibility for
social change. But it does not itself guarantee that change.

In a consciously led way, the vanguard must promote the
creation of structures that help instill new moral values, a communist attitude, in the new generations. Such a delicate process
cannot be left to chance. The vanguard should also seek to
curtail economic mechanisms, laws, and categories that lead to
new reforms and new retreats. Even unintended repetition of
such retreats may over time create a definite trend of retreats.

Che pointed out that everything stems from the erroneous
conception that it is possible to build socialism using elements
of capitalism, without *genuinely* changing their meaning. A hybrid system is thus arrived at, culminating in a dead end. This in
turn requires new concessions to economic levers—in other
words, retreats.

Che thought that perpetuating and developing capitalist economic laws and categories prolongs the social relations of bourgeois production. This in turn, he felt, would prolong the habits
of thought and the motivations of capitalist society—even
though the concepts themselves had now been metamorphosed
under socialist forms of the ownership of the means of production. Life has proven him correct.

Generally speaking, whenever a crisis in the functioning of a
socialist economy is discussed, what usually occurs is that the
discussion revolves around economic efficiency, and it tends to
concentrate on technical and administrative aspects of the
problem. The social, political, and ideological dimensions of
the alternatives under debate are not taken up. Only the superstructure, or one part of it, is called into question. Meanwhile
the *base* remains free of all suspicion.

This error presents a danger. The superstructure can be ad-
versely affected by existing economic relations. But if this element is not analyzed in subsequent discussion surrounding a
possible transformation of the economic relations, the possibility grows dramatically that a general retreat in social consciousness will set in. History has already demonstrated this.

Che pointed to this dialectical relationship. He emphasized

that market-economy mechanisms tended to acquire a physiognomy of their own, imposing their own independent dynamic on social relations as a whole. He said the same thing was true when direct material incentives were indiscriminately and unthinkingly used as the driving force of production.

Che called direct material incentives "the great Trojan horse of socialism." They undermine the socialist system from within and lead it to new retreats in consciousness and social relations.

Che called for searching out the structures that give rise to selfishness and personal ambition, in order to eliminate them. These would be replaced by new institutions and social mechanisms capable of molding the future generations differently. This is not romanticism; rather it is the Marxist-Leninist understanding that social being determines social consciousness, and that the transformation of both can only be resolved in practice and hand in hand.

I N SHORT, Che's transitional model was not conceived in order to adapt to this reality, but to transform it.

Che's analysis did not stop here, however. It went further and described what was happening and what would occur by following the beaten track of capitalism—in particular its impact on the relationship between social being and social consciousness. He delved into this and studied the *interrelationship* of structure and superstructure.

In my book I present and analyze Che's ideas on the New Economic Policy (NEP) initiated under Lenin's leadership in the young Soviet republic in 1921.[33] Here I want to stress only that under the NEP the resulting superstructure was having an increasingly marked influence on relations of production. And the conflict provoked by creating a hybrid tended to resolve itself in favor of the superstructure, leading to new retreats.

Basing himself on Marx, Che took up the theory of value, thinking about it creatively under present-day circumstances. He perceived that the political economy of socialism had adopted this theory uncritically and had made extrapolations based on limited experiences. It had not stopped to consider the transition period in sufficient depth. This shortcoming is one of the main reasons for the incorrectness, dogmatism, superficial analysis, scholasticism, inconsistent pragmatism, and schematism that characterize what increasingly came to be presented as the political economy of socialism following Lenin's death.

Che probed deeply into these questions. As a result of serious and scientific study of the NEP period, he presented a totally new and original vision based on the principles and specific elements of Marxist theory.

Che and Fidel possess the merit of having pointed out these deficiencies twenty-five years ago. Che in particular indicated the source of these follies. And he characterized, pointed to, and enumerated the principles and foundations on which political economy must be developed in the transition to socialism.

I N THE PAGES above we have pointed out the harm that has been done and continues to be done when a nation tries to use the dull instruments of capitalism to build socialism.[34] Che did not stop here; he carried his analysis over to economic relations and international policies. And in his writings and speeches he describes in detail the harm already done on the international level through the use of these instruments.

He foresaw that employing the economic accounting system in an individual country undermined the cohesiveness of the socialist camp as a whole by exacerbating individualism, selfishness, and nationalism. This seriously endangers internationalist consciousness and its effective practice, both among the socialist countries themselves as well as in their relations with the underdeveloped world.

Through speeches by Che at various international forums, the leadership of the Cuban revolution raised for the first time the injustice of unequal trade and the foreign debt.[35]

I can add to what is presented in my book only that trade between socialist countries cannot be governed by the law of value. In trade with a developed socialist country, the determination of a *just* price must take into consideration the true costs of a developing socialist country's social labor. This is because the real foundation of value is in the expenditure of physical and mental energy by the producer in the process of production, of creating value. The problems of productivity and labor intensity are elements derived from this. Although important, they can be separated from the process of expending social labor. In the end, this process is the foundation of every creation of value and wealth.

It would be timely and fitting to analyze how in practice this trade is carried out at the present time and to what degree it corresponds with Marxist-Leninist principles.

Che is part of the present

Minimizing the differences between the budgetary finance and economic accounting systems might seem logical. This is especially the case if the question is not studied in sufficient depth. But a detailed analysis of the contradictions between the two systems leads to a different conclusion: the underlying problems cannot be resolved simply by indiscriminately grafting elements of one system onto the other.

It should not be forgotten that the budgetary finance system created by Che "is part of a general conception of the development of building socialism and must therefore be studied in its totality."[36]

Che once commented on the capabilities of the budgetary finance system and the economic accounting system in terms of prioritizing material or moral incentives. He noted that the budgetary finance system could move forward with a partial use of material incentives, if so desired. But a combination of "moral incentives with financial self-management is impossible; before it even takes a couple of steps the system will get tangled in its own feet and fall on its face."[37]

One cannot attribute to Che—even partially—ideas and systems that are foreign to his way of thinking and acting.

Studying Che's thought and action has nothing to do with celebrating and/or commemorating one more anniversary. It is not a conjunctural matter. The hour of rectification is also the hour of Che.

Che is not part of the past. His thought and action are not limited in application solely to the concrete conditions of the early years of the revolution. Nor is Che just for the future. He was not simply the architect of a more perfect system of ideas, of a more perfect society, one closer to communism.

I submit that Che is part of the present, *our present*. Because if we want the men and women of today to begin to be like Che, if we want our children to become the new men and new women of the twenty-first century, we must begin by understanding that Che is first of all a man of the twentieth century, and that his ideas were intended for this century, for beginning to create today the human being of tomorrow.

In his remarks on October 8, 1987, Fidel showed with impeccable logic how correct Che had been in his thought and action. He called on our young people, our economists, our students, our cadres in the party and state—on our entire people—to study and absorb Che's political and economic thought.

Fidel said this was an absolute necessity for the development of our political education, for combating disorientation, blind imitation of and intoxication with one single type of ideas. He said it was absolutely necessary if we are to become more alert and more consistent revolutionaries, if we are going to find new solutions to problems both old and new. "I want our people to become a people of ideas, of concepts," Fidel said. "I want them to analyze those ideas, think about them, and, if they want, discuss them."[38]

We should always remember Che's words in his notes on "Socialism and Man in Cuba": "Socialism is young and has its mistakes. We revolutionaries often lack the knowledge and intellectual daring needed to meet the task of developing the new man with methods different from the conventional ones—and the conventional methods suffer from the influences of the society that created them."[39]

THE *MILITANT*
a socialist newsweekly published in the interests of working people.

Monthly Spanish-language sister publication of the Militant

perspectiva **mundial**

News and analysis on . . .

◆the rightward evolution of the social policy of the Democratic and Republican parties

◆the dramatic shifts in world politics—from mounting tensions in NATO, to war in the Balkans, to U.S. aggression in the Persian Gulf, Haiti, and elsewhere

◆the socialist revolution in Cuba

◆the unfolding class struggle in South Africa

◆trade union struggles and resistance by working farmers

◆fights against cop brutality and racism, and for women's rights

◆building a world communist movement and educating for socialism

Subscribe today!
Don't miss a single issue

SPECIAL INTRODUCTORY OFFER

The Militant ◆ 12 WEEKS **$10**

Perspectiva Mundial ◆ 4 MONTHS **$6**

The Militant is also available each week at gopher://gopher.igc.apc.org:70/11/pubs/militant on the internet.

Write for subscription prices in currencies other than the U.S. dollar. The Militant/Perspectiva Mundial, 410 West St., New York, NY 10014 Fax (212) 924-6040 CompuServe: 73311,2720

THE POLITICS OF ECONOMICS

Che Guevara and Marxist continuity

by Steve Clark and Jack Barnes

E RNESTO CHE GUEVARA, one of the outstanding Marxists of the twentieth century, sought to chart a course that would allow working people to organize and to answer in practice the single biggest question of world politics: How can we rid the world of capitalism—with its exploitation, dog-eat-dog individualism, wars, racism, oppression of women, and economic and social crises—and effect a transition toward a communist society free of these horrors? Thus, his political contributions, some of which are discussed in the three preceding articles, are important today not only for the workers and farmers of Cuba, with whom, correctly, his contributions are most closely identified; these contributions are also vital for the toiling majority of humanity and the revolutionists of action everywhere who are its vanguard.

The transition toward socialism was initiated more than seventy years ago with the victory of the October 1917 revolution in Russia. Under the leadership of the Bolshevik Party, the workers and peasants overthrew the state apparatus of the previous landlord-capitalist regimes. The Bolsheviks then mobilized the toilers to work together with the newly formed workers' and peasants' republic to expropriate the landlords and capitalists. The Bolsheviks built a new toilers' army to defend their conquests; launched an international communist movement to aid fellow workers and farmers around the world in emulating their struggle; and initiated the enormous political effort to construct the economic and social foundations to begin the transition to socialism.

Steve Clark is managing editor of New International. *Jack Barnes is national secretary of the Socialist Workers Party.*

The Soviet workers' and peasants' government initiated a radical land reform; expropriated capitalist property in industry, banking, and wholesale trade; established a state monopoly of foreign trade; and led a campaign to establish workers' control of industry and advance on that basis toward workers' management. These steps made it possible for the working class and its vanguard to begin economic planning and marked the accomplishment of a historic task—the establishment of a workers' state, the dictatorship of the proletariat. Such steps are necessary for the revolutionary toilers to begin building socialism. In and of themselves, however, they cannot guarantee a continued advance toward socialism.

In Cuba the social transformation in property relations and the establishment of a workers' state was carried out at the opening of the 1960s under a revolutionary leadership whose best-known central figure after Fidel Castro was Ernesto Che Guevara. Guevara was an Argentine who had originally trained as a physician and had joined the Castro-led July 26 Movement and the initial cadres of the Rebel Army in Mexico in the mid-1950s. At the time of the victory over the U.S.-backed Batista dictatorship in 1959, Guevara was thirty years old.

A workers' state presides over a transitional society. Having thrown off the domination of the capitalist mode of production, it initially inherits the social relations of production from that prior system of exploitation, oppression, and fierce competition among workers over jobs, promotions, and economic advantage. Depending on the caliber of its political leadership, on the size and experience of the working class, and on the pace of advances or setbacks in the world revolution, a workers' state can go *forward* toward socialism and in the process establish new social relations; or—as in the case of the horribly deformed workers' states in the Soviet Union, Eastern Europe, and China today—*backward* toward laying the social basis for the counter-revolutionary restoration of capitalism, as it reinforces the values and norms of bourgeois social relations. In fact, as the history of the past six decades has illustrated, these transitional societies can sink well below the highest points of human culture reached under bourgeois democracy.

If the dictatorship of the proletariat is not based on new social relations of production, neither is it the "first stage of socialism." Humanity's socialist future will begin only with the completion of the world revolution, which will usher in the kind of international cooperation among working people that can qualitatively surpass the productivity of human labor achieved by the industrially advanced capitalist societies.[1]

THE SHARPENING contradictions of a world still dominated by capitalism in the closing decade of the twentieth century amply confirm the burning need to advance the worldwide struggle for national liberation and socialism:

• As this article was being written, for example, Washington unleashed a murderous war against Iraq—the first of those the imperialists will launch in the 1990s as the decline of their own system drives them toward wider world conflict.

• It has become increasingly clear that world capitalism cannot "help" the privileged bureaucratic caste in Moscow reverse the deepening economic and social crisis in the USSR, which is propelling the Soviet regime in a more and more brutal Bonapartist direction. Nor can the capitalists bring economic and social stability to the Eastern European countries where Stalinist-led bureaucratic apparatuses calling themselves Communist disintegrated in late 1989 and 1990.

• The growing instability of the world's capitalist economies makes increasingly inevitable a deep international depression and devastating social crisis in coming years—and an extension of the effects of economic recession, class polarization, cop brutality, and corruption that mark the imperialist countries today. Already the majority of workers and peasants in Africa, the Americas, and capitalist Asia—debt slaves to international finance capital—are suffering under depression conditions worse than any since the 1930s.

Those who reject Guevara's fundamental proposals have long argued that while his course may be applicable to humanity's distant communist future, policies modeled on those of the regimes in the Soviet Union and Eastern Europe—that is, reformed and improved variants of those policies—are what's

ENDNOTES FOR THIS ARTICLE BEGIN ON PAGE 190.

possible and adequate to advance economic productivity and social progress in today's world. But the disastrous consequences of the existing variants of the "Soviet model" are now plain for all to see.

All these bureaucratically deformed workers' states, without exception, had for decades been moving further away from socialism, not toward it. That fact has now been settled by history. Today the burden of proof rests not with those who advocate Guevara's communist course—a course consistent with that charted under Lenin's leadership in the early years of the Communist International, and true to the liberating perspectives opened by the Cuban revolution—but with those who claim that some variant of what was tried by Stalin or his successors in the Soviet Union and Eastern Europe can lead toward socialism.

Guevara and Cuba's rectification process
The articles by Mary-Alice Waters, Carlos Rafael Rodríguez, and Carlos Tablada are part of a discussion that has been under way in Cuba and internationally for several years. That discussion centers on the place of Guevara's contributions to what in Cuba is called the rectification process. The leadership of the Communist Party of Cuba initiated the rectification process in April 1986, following the first session of the party's Third Congress. Their objective was a concerted effort to reverse the accumulating negative consequences of the retreat accelerated in the mid-1970s by the growing application of methods of organizing the economy and basic leadership institutions borrowed from the Soviet Union and the Eastern European regimes. The broad sweep of the rectification process itself grew out of two years of work by the Cuban leadership to reorganize and reestablish political control over the economic planning bureaucracy, which had increasingly diverged from the priorities set by the highest government bodies.[2]

What made it possible in Cuba to catch and attempt to rectify the dangerous and retrograde trends fostered by the policies adopted in the mid-1970s is the fact that the central leadership in the government and Communist Party remains in the hands of a revolutionary cadre. The relatively privileged technocratic and petty-bourgeois layers that bloat the apparatus of state, party, and other institutions have proven unable to impose their anti-working-class perspectives and interests on the political course of the revolution—an outcome that could be achieved only by driving the workers and peasants out of political life and activity. They have not succeeded in reversing Cuba's revolutionary internationalism and substituting some form of "national socialism," whose strategy revolves around concessions aimed at producing a live-and-let-live accommodation with U.S. imperialism instead of active solidarity with the fighting vanguard of the oppressed and exploited worldwide.

In an October 1987 speech marking the twentieth anniversary of Guevara's assassination, Fidel Castro pointed out that throughout the three decades of the Cuban revolution "no serious attempt was ever made to put [Guevara's proposals] into practice, and there came a time when ideas diametrically opposed to Che's economic thought began to take over."[3] The effort to understand, reconquer, and apply Guevara's political contributions today, Castro emphasized, is central to the struggle for further advances in Cuba.

WAS CASTRO being impractical in stressing that "many of Che's ideas are absolutely relevant today, ideas without which I am convinced communism cannot be built"?[4] Or was he accurately pointing toward the central challenge lying ahead for the vanguard of the working class in Cuba? Those questions stake out the poles of the wide-ranging discussion inside and outside Cuba concerning Guevara's political legacy and its applicability to Cuban society today.

Carlos Tablada, in his 1989 article "The Creativity of Che's Economic Thought," published here in English for the first time, presents the view that "Che is not part of the past. His thought and action are not limited in application solely to the concrete conditions of the early years of the revolution. Nor is Che just for the future. He was not simply the architect of a more perfect system of ideas, of a more perfect society, one closer to communism." Instead, Tablada insists, "Che is part of the present, *our present.*"

"The hour of rectification," Tablada points out, "is also the hour of Che."

The course Guevara advocated and sought to implement as part of the leadership of the revolution in its early years cannot be reduced to what is usually thought of as "economics." Instead, he concentrated his energies on what might more accurately be called the *politics of economics.*

Guevara's aim was not to come up with ways to administer economic production and distribution, approaching the working class from the outside, as one "input" or "factor of production" (albeit the most important one, the "human factor," as Stalinist-trained economists often put it). The goal was to organize and raise the political consciousness of workers, enabling us to exercise growing control over the economic and social decisions that simultaneously shape production and our own lives. The aim was to increase workers' powers to determine society's collective needs, as well as conscious command over the allocation of labor and resources to meet them. Through this effort, working people would transform their own values and attitudes; their creativity and imagination would begin to be freed from the stunting and alienating conditions of life and work under capitalist social relations.

Guevara PLACED the development of ever greater technical and administrative skills, voluntary labor, political consciousness and participation, and the self-transformation of working people at the center of revolutionizing the social relations of production and exchange. The course he advocated was the opposite of a policy that—in the name of "greater efficiency"—relies on a state planning bureaucracy to *administer* the producers, while it "provides" them a broader social welfare net. Such a course, he was convinced, would only demobilize, depoliticize, and demoralize working people, thereby erecting the ultimate barrier to advances in the productivity of human labor.

The task of the revolutionary government and its communist leadership, Guevara held, is to create organizational forms that increasingly draw the working class into competent administration and management of economic enterprises and into informed decision-making on the social and political priorities of the workers' state. From this standpoint, for Guevara the acid test of any system of economic planning and management was whether it advanced or set back this line of march—the only road toward socialism and communism.

Guevara explicitly counterposed this Marxist approach to the views presented in contemporary economic manuals produced in the Soviet Union, all of which took as their starting point Stalin's 1952 booklet *Economic Problems of Socialism in the U.S.S.R.* There Stalin argued that the key to the transition to socialism was to "get to know" the laws of motion of capitalism (such as the law of value) in order to "master them, learn to apply them with full understanding, utilize them in the interests of society, and thus subjugate them, secure mastery over them."[5]

Stalin's heirs took this negation of the foundations of Marxism for a "theoretical breakthrough" and pushed it a step further, frequently elevating the law of value to the status of a universal law of social development. This conveniently provided a scientific-sounding rationalization for the increasing social inequality between the privileged caste dominating the state and party apparatus in the Soviet Union and the vast majority of workers and peasants, as well as for the increasing social differentiation within the working class itself.

Guevara explicitly polemicized against this view that building socialism is a task of administrators adept in manipulating laws and mechanisms inherited from capitalism. Instead, he insisted, it is a revolutionary task based on advancing the political consciousness and collective experience of the working class, as the blind laws of capitalism wither away.

The 1963-64 debate in Cuba

In 1963-64 Guevara took a prominent part in a public debate in several Cuban journals on alternative perspectives on the organization of the Cuban economy. The discussion focused on contrasting evaluations of two approaches to economic planning and management being implemented simultaneously in Cuba in those years.

Guevara advocated what was called the budgetary system for financing state enterprises ("budgetary finance system" for short). Under the budgetary finance system, these enterprises were financed centrally by the state bank from funds budgeted in accordance with the national economic plan and state planning agencies. Enterprises had no funds of their own to use at their individual discretion. Money relations between the enterprise and state bank, and among state enterprises themselves, were simply accounting procedures to monitor implementation of the state plan and establish indexes to reflect the relative costs of goods produced by various enterprises (and trace their trends up or down).

"In a budgetary system, with properly functioning systems of controls and supervision," Guevara wrote, "there is no need for the bank to be involved in investment decisions. These are political decisions concerning economic policy that are in the purview of the state's Central Planning Board. . . . The bank should concern itself with scrutinizing fund withdrawals according to proper procedure, which is its specific function."[6]

The alternative "economic accounting system" was in use in enterprises organized by the National Institute of Agrarian Reform, then headed by Carlos Rafael Rodríguez, as well as in those accountable to the Ministry of Foreign Trade, directed by Alberto Mora. This was a method of planning and management, adopted from the Soviet Union and Eastern European countries, that relied substantially on use of capitalist market mechanisms, profit criteria, and material incentives. Under that system, state enterprises retained their own funds, out of which they financed expenditures and investments in line with broad targets set out in the state economic plan. (This system was thus also referred to as "financial self-management.") Transactions among state enterprises were organized on the basis of money payments, and enterprises took loans at interest from the state bank to carry on their operations and expand. As a result, the money "profits" of an individual enterprise, and credit and interest policies of the state bank, played a substantial role in determining economic priorities.

Guevara wrote several contributions to this debate. In one of them—his reply to "On the Operation of the Law of Value in the Cuban Economy" by Alberto Mora, the minister of foreign trade —Guevara opened by underlining how important it was that such an exchange of views be conducted on the basis of the greatest possible clarity, political objectivity, and openness, rather than in Aesopian language or hidden polemics. (Guevara's reply to Mora is reprinted elsewhere in this issue.) Guevara wrote:

The article [by Mora] begins by saying: "Some comrades contend that the law of value no longer functions within the state sector of the Cuban economy." Refuting arguments is important, but identifying those who hold the viewpoint being challenged is also important. "Some comrades" have neither first names nor last names. But the individuals to whom the critique is directed do. They are the minister of industry [Guevara], who is the author of this article, and Comrade Luis Alvarez Rom, the minister of finance—not to mention others who, as part of the current supporting the budgetary finance system, may also be intended as targets of criticism.

Guevara returned to this theme in the concluding paragraphs of his article:

> With our reply, a polemic is now under way. Polemics can be of considerable educational value so long as we conduct them with the greatest possible scientific rigor and objectivity. We do not shy away from confrontations. But since we are in the midst of a discussion that involves the highest levels of the government and party, where two schools of thought exist regarding the system of financing, we feel that careful attention to the form and method of the discussion is important.

IN APRIL 1965 Guevara left Cuba to help lead revolutionary struggles abroad. During the latter half of the year he was in the Congo (now Zaire) to assist supporters of slain Prime Minister Patrice Lumumba in their struggle against the reactionary regime imposed there by U.S. and Belgian imperialism. In 1966 he went to Bolivia. There he led a guerrilla detachment seeking to mount a revolutionary struggle against that country's military dictatorship and help give an impulse to the revolutionary struggle in the increasingly explosive Southern Cone of the Americas (Argentina, Chile, and Uruguay). In October 1967 Guevara was wounded, captured, and subsequently murdered by U.S.-organized Bolivian troops.

Following Guevara's departure from Cuba, others in the Ministry of Industry, various state planning agencies, and the leadership of the Communist Party itself began to apply leftist policies that—although never advocated by Guevara—were nonetheless advanced under the banner of the budgetary finance system or Guevara's "thought." In 1968, for example, all small private retailers in Cuba—including some 3,700 street vendors—had their shops expropriated and placed under state ownership. Major new investments in industrial enterprises and economic infrastructure in Cuba began to be made with little or no attention to the cost accounting and budgetary controls considered so vital by Guevara to be able to accurately judge expenditures of labor, raw materials, and foreign currency.

As CASTRO NOTED in his October 1987 speech, blame for these leftist policies tended to be placed at the door of the budgetary finance system. Some of Che's ideas were "incorrectly interpreted and, what's more, incorrectly applied," Castro said, referring to this period.[7]

Carlos Rafael Rodríguez also underlines the incorrectness of equating Guevara's course with the erroneous policies of this period. "One of the biggest heresies committed in this country," says Rodríguez, "was to suppose that what we were doing from 1967 to 1970—the lack of economic controls that prevailed in those years—could be carried out, as some did, in the name of Che Guevara." Rodríguez labels such claims "unjust" and "antihistorical" and adds: "I remember that some of our institutions brought out pamphlets containing what was alleged to be the thought of Che Guevara, but which in reality was the *mutilated* thought of Che Guevara."

This period culminated in 1970 in the failure of the all-out drive to harvest and process ten million tons of sugarcane. The plan was, by a heroic effort of will, to increase output to its highest level in Cuban history in order to obtain the resources necessary to accelerate Cuba's industrial development. As it turned out, the yield fell short by 1.5 million tons. Although the 8.5 million tons harvested was itself a record, the entire fabric of production in Cuba had been disrupted by lack of attention to other agricultural and industrial priorities. Moral exhortation and enthusiasm had been permitted to falsely parade as an application of Guevara's policies of voluntary labor and of organizing production and incentives to promote rather than retard communist consciousness and collective action by working people.

In the aftermath of this failure, Fidel Castro and the leadership of the government and Communist Party took responsibility for its consequences. Nonetheless, these leftist errors further tipped the scales in Cuba away from any serious efforts to build on Guevara's contributions. This played into the hands of the slowly growing layers in Cuba who were succumbing to disappointment, tiredness, and the temptations of privilege under the pressures of repeated failures of revolutionary developments in the Americas to culminate in new workers' and farmers' governments. Guevara's own efforts in Bolivia had been defeated. The revolutionary opportunities of a wave of guerrilla struggles in Latin America had largely been exhausted by the end of the decade. Pinochet's 1973 military coup in Chile and beheading of the revolutionary vanguard there signaled the coming exhaustion of another set of potential revolutionary openings, this time in the Southern Cone. With the rightist coup in Argentina in 1976, the bloody suppression of the rebels in the Southern Cone had been completed.

The strains inside Cuba as a result of these setbacks were among the factors that fostered the turn in the early 1970s toward greater reliance on methods borrowed from the Soviet Union and Eastern Europe, the negative results of which are now being combated through the rectification process. This shift in course was ratified at the 1975 congress of the Communist Party of Cuba by adoption of the Economic Management and Planning System, based on the principles of the economic accounting system (increased reliance on enterprise profitability and other market-oriented criteria, individual money incentives, etc.). The Economic Management and Planning System—referred to as "a lame nag with many sores" by Fidel Castro in his October 1987 speech on Guevara—remains in effect in Cuba today.[8]

Over the next decade, from 1975 through the mid-1980s, the individual aspects of Guevara's political legacy that were carried over into the new system eroded (and were corrupted in the process). This was the case with collective voluntary labor, on which Guevara had placed great importance in promoting a new attitude toward work on the part of working people. As workers took increasing command of economic administration and political decision-making, Guevara explained, they would be increasingly motivated to work for the benefit of society, both in Cuba and worldwide, not just for themselves and their families.

At the beginning of the 1970s, Guevara's approach toward voluntary work was institutionalized with the launching of the minibrigades—groups of workers who volunteer to be released from their regular jobs for a period of time to work on various socially needed construction projects, such as schools, day-care facilities, housing, clinics, hospitals, bakeries, and shopping and recreational centers. Following adoption of the Economic Management and Planning System in 1975, however, the minibrigades were all but abandoned.

In Castro's October 1987 speech he explained that "voluntary work, the brainchild of Che . . . was steadily on the decline. . . . The bureaucrat's view, the technocrat's view that voluntary work was neither basic nor essential gained more and more ground."[9]

The budgetary finance system that Che Guevara sought to implement was not only an approach to the organization of the labor of workers and farmers that would reinforce the development of new social relations based on collective effort and human solidarity. Guevara was also convinced this was the only way over time to make best use of society's resources and raise the productivity of human labor.

The budgetary finance system aimed at creating an integrated and centralized national structure of economic enterprises. This would provide greater leverage for the working class to exercise decision making over economic and social priorities in allocating labor and resources to various sectors of production. The budgetary finance system sought to promote growing workers' control in the factories as a road toward increasing working-class management and administration of these economic enterprises. To the degree this course was advanced, it would also give added impetus and content to workers' democracy through the political structures of the workers' state (such as the local, provincial, and national assemblies of People's Power initiated in Cuba in the mid-1970s).

As part of the budgetary finance system, Guevara sought to

structure wage incentives to encourage workers to broaden their education and upgrade their skills. He recognized the need to break down the social division of labor between production workers and administrative personnel by organizing the work force to take on—bit by bit—additional aspects of supervision, bookkeeping, cost accounting, inventory monitoring, and other tasks reserved under capitalism exclusively to the employer. Within the framework of the budgetary finance system, Guevara encouraged the application of the most advanced techniques of accounting, industrial technology, and work organization developed by capitalism, including computerization.

THE BUDGETARY FINANCE system aimed to promote new, communist attitudes toward work that develop as we exercise initiative in a socially productive manner to accomplish explicit goals that are justified politically and are set collectively. Central to advancing along this course were steps to reduce social inequalities in the working class, including the special forms of discrimination and prejudice inherited from the horrors of capitalist and precapitalist social systems—racist discrimination, the oppression of women, superexploitation of rural toilers, and mind-deadening isolated individual labor.

As working people organized in this way to transform the economic foundations of society, raising the level of social labor productivity, Guevara was convinced they would at the same time be transforming their own consciousness—their own socially determined and changing "human nature." That's why he placed such importance on voluntary labor, as well as on internationalist solidarity with workers and farmers in struggle the world over.

Without advancing along these lines, socialist planning is impossible. The building of socialism cannot take place spontaneously, without leadership, without a working class increasingly imbued with a historical and internationalist world outlook. The course advocated by Guevara, and embodied in the budgetary finance system, assumed the existence of a strong, growing, and increasingly proletarian communist party, composed of the most committed, politically conscious, self-sacrifing, and internationalist vanguard of the working class.

Can capitalist laws be 'used'?

The article by Carlos Rafael Rodríguez on "Che's Contribution to the Cuban Economy" is of particular interest since, as he notes:

> Much has been written abroad—even whole books—about differences of opinion Che may have had with one or another comrade, and I in particular have been singled out. I am proud to say that while we did have some differences, we always viewed things identically with regard to fundamental economic questions. We worked together, along with other comrades, to impose a little order in the Cuban economy, to attain the maximum efficiency in the Cuban economy, and to establish something that is essential—whatever one's starting point: and that is implementation of controls over the economy.

In reviewing the contributions by Guevara that he believes should be given greater emphasis in economic planning and management in Cuba, Rodríguez also points to several positions on which he differs with Guevara's views. In this regard, Rodríguez's article represents the clearest and most considered presentation of a viewpoint on Guevara's contributions that is quite widely held both inside and outside Cuba. Taking a closer look at some of these points of disagreement can help clarify the unfolding discussion.

The first issue on which Rodríguez states a difference with Guevara is of fundamental importance: that is, whether or not the laws of motion of capitalism—once clearly understood by the political leadership of a workers' state—can then be used by it as tools to advance the construction of socialism. Rodríguez says:

> Che did not pose elimination of the law of value as an absolute. It is worthwhile to recall this, since we acknowledge that the law of value continues to operate and has certain effects. What Che said was that the law of value could not be the guiding principle of economic activity. He said that as a result of the conditions created by social-

ism we are able to manipulate the law of value, to use it to benefit socialism. . . .

The issue is not absolute defense of the law of value, of the inevitability of the market. . . . At issue is controlled utilization of the law of value, taking into account the circumstances imposed by Cuba's current economic reality and historic conditions.

Guevara himself, however, presented his view somewhat differently. Perhaps the most succinct presentation is contained in his February 1964 article "Planning and Consciousness in the Transition to Socialism ('On the Budgetary Finance System')."[10] There, Guevara took issue with the *Manual of Political Economy* published in the Soviet Union. He pointed to "a profound difference" between his views and "that of proponents of economic accounting regarding the concept of the law of value and the possibility of using it consciously." According to the Soviet handbook, Guevara explained, "The law of value would act as a blind force, but once it is understood it can be handled, or used, by man."[11]

Guevara disagreed with this judgment: "We reject the possibility of consciously using the law of value in the absence of a free market that automatically expresses the contradiction between producers and consumers."[12] He thus rejected the possibility of "controlled utilization of the law of value."

WHAT IS AT issue in these contrasting approaches?

The dictatorship of the proletariat—the transitional society that is inaugurated by the expropriation of big capital in industry, mining, transportation, banking, and wholesale trade—has no blind laws of motion of its own. Its advance toward socialism can be the product only of *conscious political action* by the organized workers and farmers, using their government, its related economic institutions, and other mass organizations (trade unions, organizations of farmers, women, youth, and oppressed nationalities). The working class must more and more become the "planners" of the planned economy. This process must be led by a communist party that is increasingly the vanguard of the most committed, active, and politically conscious working people, first and foremost from the industrial working class.

The only economic laws that continue to operate during this transition period are the blind laws of commodity markets (the "law of value") carried over from the prior capitalist society. These laws continue to operate directly inside the country wherever markets exist, as well as indirectly through the workers' state's ongoing involvement in trade on the world market. These laws will wither away only as commodity production and exchange themselves disappear; there are sharp limits on the degree to which this can occur in any one country or handful of countries, since the level of development of society's productive forces must undergo a qualitative advance that is possible only on the basis of the extension of the world socialist revolution and growing international economic progress and cooperation.

Like other Marxist giants before him—from Marx and Engels through Bolshevik leaders of the Soviet republic such as V.I. Lenin and Leon Trotsky—Guevara recognized the reality that commodity relations cannot be "abolished" or "suppressed" during the transition to socialism.

THE LAW OF VALUE continues to operate, above all in sectors of the economy where small-scale commodity production still exists (peasant farms in the countryside, agricultural and handicraft cooperatives, small shops), as well as in the exchange of consumer goods between individuals and state enterprises. "We consider the law of value to be partially operative because remnants of the commodity society still exist," Guevara wrote in the February 1964 article. "This is also reflected in the type of exchange that takes place between the state as supplier and the consumer."[13]

Commodity relations, however, should not be equated with *capitalist* relations. Commodity relations and markets existed for thousands of years prior to the rise of capitalism, and to that extent the law of value operated during that entire historical period.[14]

Industrial capitalism, however, came into existence only at the point in history (in the mid-1700s) when commodity production and exchange began to be increasingly generalized and dominant on the basis of private ownership of industry, banking, and wholesale trade—when crossing the bridge from manufacturing to machinofacturing became possible.[15] Rodríguez slides over this decisive distinction between commodity relations and capitalist relations when he refers to the transition to socialism as "the period in which, *while slowly leaving capitalism behind,* we are building socialism as fast as we can" (emphasis added).

But it is not capitalism that is slowly left behind in a country during the transition to socialism. Capitalism can and must be *abolished* in order to create the conditions to even begin building socialism. That task of abolition is accomplished with the expropriation by a workers' and farmers' government of capitalist property in industry, mining, major transportation, banking, and wholesale trade, and the establishment of a state monopoly of foreign trade. Only these steps open the door to the kind of economic planning by the working class that can lead toward socialism. That door was opened in the Soviet republic in 1918 and in Cuba in the second half of 1960.

These revolutionary anticapitalist measures break the domination of the specific form of the law of value characteristic under capitalism: the establishment of prices of production through the competition of large capitals, determining an average rate of profit and apportioning a share of surplus value to particular individual capitals proportionate to their size. Under capitalism, these prices of production regulate the social allocation of labor, raw materials, and production goods among various sectors of the economy, and guarantee the growing together of industrial capital and banking and the reproduction and domination of bourgeois social relations, the inequitable distribution of wealth and income, and political rule by a relative handful of economically powerful bourgeois families.

Accordingly, when big capital is expropriated, the anarchic competition that determines such allocations under capitalism can be consciously replaced with planned production and distribution in line with social priorities and needs that have been discussed and decided by working people.

These considerations make it clear, for example, why it would have been a leftist error to have advocated any short-term perspective of establishing a workers' state in Burkina Faso during the period (1983-87) when a revolutionary popular government existed there under the leadership of Thomas Sankara, a revolutionary and communist of the highest caliber. Economic and social relations in that country were characterized to such a degree by small-scale commodity production, and capitalist relations of production and exchange were so relatively undeveloped, that the expropriation of the small-scale industrial and banking sector could not have given the revolutionary government sufficient leverage to determine the overall direction of social and economic priorities and development.[16]

This was not the case for Cuba at the opening of the 1960s, however, despite the relative backwardness of its economic and social conditions as a semicolonial country oppressed by imperialism (relative, that is, to the imperialist countries). The character of industry, banking, communications, freight transportation, and large-scale agriculture and processing in Cuba was such that capitalist development was shaped by prices of production, and the productive apparatus could thus begin to be submitted to conscious political decision by the toilers once these big capitals were expropriated by the revolutionary government.

A WORKERS' STATE during the transition to socialism, moreover, does not need to wait for the gradual withering away of commodity relations with regard to every aspect of small-scale production and consumption goods and services. The workers' and farmers' government can and must set social priorities that involve eliminating commodity relations in some sectors in order to advance such goals as redressing gross social inequalities and raising the living conditions of the working class as a whole.

In Cuba, for example, health care and education have for decades not been commodities bought and sold on the market and thus available only to those from better-off families able to afford these services. Instead, schooling and medical attention are guaranteed free of charge as a right of all. Since the opening years of the revolution, affordable housing has been a guaranteed right of all Cubans. A cap has been placed on housing rent, which can generally be no more than 10 percent of the head of the household's income.[17] Prices of basic food items and other necessities are subsidized and provided to all Cubans, in the quantities available and on an equitable basis. Employment is guaranteed (or a living income during a period of training or a transition between jobs).

With regard to family farmers and farm cooperatives, the revolutionary government centralizes the purchase of agricultural commodities and places limits on the price of foodstuffs sold to Cuban working people. At the same time, the government guarantees needed agricultural inputs (seed, fertilizer, tools, etc.), cheap credit, and a living income to small-scale farmers and members of farm cooperatives. Land is no longer a commodity; it cannot be bought and sold on the market or mortgaged, sinking the farmer into debt slavery to a bank or other lender.

The pace at which these particular aspects of commodity relations can be broken by a workers' state will be limited by the level and character of economic development of a particular country. At the same time, so long as social inequality exists (let alone sharpens) during the period of the transition to socialism, there will be a tendency for a "black market" to grow up in all these goods and services parallel to what the revolutionary government is able to provide. This creates a social milieu in which parasitic petty-bourgeois layers operate and seek to increase their influence throughout the apparatus of the state, party, trade unions, and other institutions.

Commodity relations between state enterprises

Even after the expropriation of capitalist industry and banking, it is still possible for blindly determined prices of production to begin to be reproduced and to determine—beyond any conscious decision and control by working people—the economic and social investment priorities of a workers' state.

This tendency is inevitable if relations among state enterprises are conducted on a commodity basis—that is, if state enterprises (1) are forced into competitive markets to purchase needed raw materials, machinery, semifinished products, and other inputs, and (2) set the prices and find their own markets for the finished goods they produce. (To varying degrees, these procedures have prevailed for decades under the economic accounting system in the Soviet Union and Eastern Europe. In Cuba they were generalized under the Economic Management and Planning System in the mid-1970s.)

If the allocation of labor time, raw materials, semifinished goods, machinery, construction materials, and freight transport is established in this way, it is impossible to organize economic and social planning that diminishes the sway of the laws of motion of capitalism and leads toward socialism. Under such conditions, each enterprise functions increasingly on the basis of its own "profitability" rather than in line with a centralized national plan to advance social and political priorities.

This is in fact what began to occur more and more in Cuba following implementation of the Economic Management and Planning System. Since late 1984 when the reorientation got under way that two years later led to the rectification process, leaders of the Communist Party of Cuba have pointed to many of the negative consequences of this trend. As Fidel Castro explained in a May 1987 interview with the French Communist Party's daily newspaper, *L'Humanité:*

> Numerous plants tried to be profitable by charging high prices—real robbery. They didn't try to become profitable by improving efficiency or by reducing energy or labor costs. They even earned money at the expense of other plants. . . .
>
> We already began to see contradictions arising between the interests of certain enterprises and those of society, as well as tendencies to earn more by producing more, but of poorer quality.[18]

It was in order to combat such a reimposition of the tyranny of capitalist laws and methods that Guevara rejected the use "of the *commodity* category in relations between state enterprises. We consider all such establishments to be part of the single large enterprise that is the state" (emphasis in original), he explained in his February 1964 article on the budgetary finance system.[19]

Rodríguez has a contrary view from Guevara's on this question, as well. "To be sure, we could do away with the category of commodity and view the product simply as one element of exchange within one big enterprise, the state," says Rodríguez. "But that, in our opinion, leads to even greater difficulties than if the products are considered commodities to be bought and sold by the enterprises."

Rodríguez acknowledges that "the idea that what is good for an enterprise is good for the economy is only partially true. The enterprise is a producer of resources, a supplier of resources. . . . But in order for the enterprise to work for the benefit of the economy," he says, "the enterprise's plan, its investments, even the assortment of its products . . . must be decided, in their fundamentals, in a centralized way."

But it is just this centralized planning, Guevara pointed out, that becomes impossible for the working class to organize if the relations between state enterprises are commodity relations. Instead, such functioning inevitably breeds corner-cutting disregard for quality, price gouging justified by cost accounting, speculative hoarding of raw materials, spare parts, and inventories, and all the other symptoms of bureaucratic mismanagement that mark most enterprises and institutions in the Stalinist-dominated workers' states.

CОММОDITY RELATIONS among state enterprises is the meat and potatoes of growing layers of careerists in management and administrative positions who are primarily motivated by improving their own family's conditions of life. (As Mary-Alice Waters notes in her article in this issue of *New International,* the size of factory administrations relative to the productive work force ballooned enormously in Cuba following adoption of the Economic Management and Planning System. Managerial and supervisory personnel in some cases outnumbered production workers and technicians. Measures to reduce these bloated administrative layers have been undertaken in recent years, not only in economic enterprises but also in the state and party apparatus itself.)

The operation of state enterprises on this basis exacerbates competition among workers and breaks down solidarity in the working class, at home and worldwide. The interests of workers in one enterprise are increasingly pitted against those of other enterprises, and thus of society as a whole. Corruption and privilege seeking spreads among management personnel eager to secure a base for themselves and among growing layers of workers as well. Trade unions—which Lenin said should serve as a "school of communism" for the working class during the dictatorship of the proletariat[20]—instead degenerate into mutual protection societies to provide cover for the breakdown of work norms, for wage and bonus payments with less and less relationship to hours worked and quality of output, and for loss of interest in promoting the interests of the workers of the world as a whole. Inequalities between town and country are reinforced, as well as between more and less economically developed regions of the country. Progress in eradicating the material foundations of racist and sexist divisions and prejudices within the working class is undermined. Enthusiasm for internationalist missions is sapped.

THE MINISTRY of Industry in Cuba under Guevara's leadership in the early 1960s sought to centralize transactions among its various enterprises through the state bank, which authorized and monitored disbursements in line with the state economic plan. All revenues collected by a state enterprise were deposited in a single account with those from all other state enterprises. Funds for the purchase of raw materials and renewal of equipment were withdrawn from common funds in accordance with the guidelines of the overall state plan. Semifinished products and production goods were supplied by one enterprise to another on the same centralized basis. Funds to enterprises for modernization, expansion, or technological upgrading were allocated through the national bank not to the highest bidder in terms of the interest rate competing enterprises could "afford," but once again in line with overall national targets set by state planning agencies.

Guevara advocated this approach not simply for reasons of administrative or technical efficiency (although he firmly believed that the limited historical evidence at hand demonstrated that this approach would result in the least wasteful use of labor, resources, and machinery). Instead, he recognized that only through such centralized functioning—and rejection of reliance on blind mechanisms—was it possible for the working class to progressively increase its conscious decision-making leverage and control over the economic and social priorities of the workers' state. It was along this road that workers would take on more of the functions performed by technicians and administrators—functions that would also lead toward diminishing inequalities bred by the social division of labor carried over from class-divided society. It was along this road that bureaucratization would be minimized. As Waters points out, the experiences with the vanguard construction contingents initiated as part of the rectification process speak in favor of Guevara's approach.

Thus, contrary to a frequent criticism of the budgetary finance system, it was not a recipe for bureaucratism. To the contrary, it was a strategy to assure the most rapid possible development of expanded workers' control, management, and democracy. "The system is said to have a tendency toward bureaucratism," Guevara said in the February 1964 article. "Now, from the standpoint of objective analysis, it is evident that the more we centralize all the recording and controlling operations of the enterprise or unit, the less bureaucracy there will be."[21]

Moreover, Guevara said, "It is important to point out that the general idea of mutual cooperation is being instilled in the worker, the idea of belonging to a great whole made up of the country's people. There is an impulse to the development of his consciousness of social duty."[22]

Proletarian centralism in setting economic and social priorities, and then collectively organizing to implement them in the workplace, is a powerful weapon *against* bureaucratic arbitrariness, abuse, and corruption. It is the opposite of the use of administrative, command-style methods of organization where clear lines of responsibility for decisions and their implementation disappear into a maze of bureaus. Progress toward greater solidarity and cooperation among working people is also destroyed by methods of administration and management that promote the maximization of profits by competing individual state enterprises.

Propagandists for capitalism claim that bureaucratism is somehow inherent in state property and centralized economic planning and management. But Guevara was well aware that the growth of bureaucracy was above all endemic to large capitalist enterprises and the modern bourgeois state—and the aping of their norms, values, and mechanisms by the leaderships of workers' states. Bureaucratism is the far more prevalent norm than "perfect competition" and the "free mobility of inputs" in the imperialist epoch. The various levels of government and of management of major corporations (including the banks) in the United States and other imperialist countries are both huge in size and marked by irreformable waste, sloth, corruption, and inertia. Such bureaucratism is protected and promoted by the bourgeois state. Capitalism in the 1980s and opening of the 1990s has been marked by a plethora of exposures of "white collar" millionaire and billionaire criminals (far outnumbered, of course, by their superrich counterparts, in and out of government, who remain unexposed).

Moreover, the experience in this century with the bureaucratic degeneration of the Soviet, Eastern European, and other workers' states amply confirms that the roots of administration based on methods of fiat and command in countries where the capitalist class has been expropriated are not to be found in state property and economic planning as such. To the contrary, these brutal and administrative methods flow from the political expropriation of the working class by a privileged, petty-bourgeois social caste, deeply imbued with commodity fetishism and capitalist values of self-centeredness and money hunger. The economic accounting system fosters these bourgeois attitudes, while the budgetary finance system seeks to restrict and to replace them over time with growing voluntary labor and socially conscious cooperation among free men and women.

Communist consciousness

Rodríguez argues that "Che let himself be carried away . . . [with] the view that it was possible in the short term to attain the level of consciousness of a communist society. . . . That's why he proposed eliminating in the most vigorous way possible the old categories, principally the law of value."

If this were true, it would indicate that Guevara was more utopian than communist. But Rodríguez's judgment does not seem to us to accurately present Guevara's views on the relationship between the transformation of the material foundations necessary to advance toward socialism, and the self-transformation of consciousness by working people engaged in this revolutionary activity.

"Communism is a goal of humanity that is achieved consciously," Guevara wrote in his February 1964 article on the budgetary finance system. "Therefore, education, the elimination of the vestiges of the old society in people's consciousness, is an extremely important factor. It should be kept in mind, however, that without parallel advances in production, such a society will never be achieved."[23]

GUEVARA RECOGNIZED that the laws of motion of capitalism—to the degree they persist during the transition to socialism—will by their very nature tend to reinforce capitalist social relations and bourgeois values that lead away from rather than toward socialism and communism. Thus, the operation of these capitalist laws and methods needs to be restricted and counteracted from the outset by conscious social planning and voluntary collective activity by working people.

The communist leadership must promote methods consistent with the revolution's historic goal: *the social transformation of the individual human beings* carrying out the reorganization of economic and social relations. To rely on methods inconsistent with these ends will reproduce the capitalist social relations and divisions that the revolution was made to combat and replace in the first place. It will not only block the advance toward socialism but will guarantee inefficiency, waste, corruption, class polarization, and depoliticization.

The accuracy of Guevara's judgment can be seen in trends that increasingly developed in Cuba following the turn in the early 1970s toward reliance on political rationalizations and economic methods borrowed from the Soviet Union and Eastern Europe. In October 1987 Castro remarked that were Guevara "to have seen a group of enterprises teeming with two-bit capitalists—as we call them—playing at capitalism, beginning to think and act like capitalists, forgetting about the country, the people, and high standards . . . he would have been appalled."[24] And this corrosion reached beyond administrative and managerial layers to growing sections of the working class itself, resulting in demoralization, absenteeism, routinism, lack of concern about quality—even profiteering—and the breakdown of class solidarity.

The pace of the transition to socialism was *not* the key issue for Guevara. Nor did he anywhere suggest that the consciousness, attitudes, and values that will characterize human beings in a communist society could be rapidly achieved in Cuba, or in any other single workers' state.

"We understand that the capitalist categories are retained for a time and that the length of this time cannot be determined beforehand," Guevara explained. "But the characteristics of the transition period are those of a society throwing off its old bonds in order to arrive quickly at the new stage. The *tendency* must be, in our opinion, to eliminate as vigorously as possible the old categories, including the market, money, and, therefore, the lever of material interest—or, to put it better, to eliminate the conditions for their existence."[25] Guevara speaks of *vigor*—revolutionary activity—not an unsustainable forced pace to an a priori timetable.

I N OTHER WORDS, what was central to advancing the revolution was not to somehow determine beforehand the *duration* of the transition, but to influence its *tendency* and *direction of motion* in order to attain the maximum *sustainable* pace, not a sudden burst of activity followed by exhaustion and torpor. Guevara recognized that in a world still dominated by capitalism there was no such thing as standing still during the dictatorship of the proletariat. Either the communist leadership of the vanguard of the working class would organize the toilers to move forward toward socialism or the pressures of the world market would inevitably push toward social relations more favorable to the counterrevolutionary restoration of capitalism.

Guevara insisted that a communist leadership must start organizing workers and farmers to transform social relations from the very beginning, because only in that process can working people begin fundamentally transforming their own political consciousness and attitudes. His experience in the two-year-long revolutionary war that brought down the U.S.-backed dictatorship in Cuba at the opening of 1959, his week-by-week contact and involvement with workers, farmers, and soldiers during the first years of revolutionary construction of the new Cuba, and his knowledge of the history of the revolutionary movement in Cuba and worldwide—all this gave Guevara great confidence in the capacities of ordinary men and women for hard work, human solidarity, and self-transformation. Che Guevara did not have an ounce of the cynicism of the petty-bourgeois labor bureaucrat who bitterly complains that he "doesn't have the working class he deserves."

Experience convinced Guevara that with clear, confident, and disciplined political leadership, the working class was capable of accomplishing great historic tasks. Labor productivity could be advanced. Progress could be made toward engaging in work as a social responsibility rather than simply a means of individual survival and gain. Cooperation and solidarity could be strengthened in the working class, reducing competition for jobs and promotions. The capacity to work collectively toward commonly held social ends could be increased. Affirmative action could bring forward workers—including victims of the double and triple oppression and prejudices inherited from capitalism—for training, education, and growing self-confidence and leadership responsibility in all arenas of the revolution.[26] Internationalist solidarity could gain ground over narrow nationalist, family, and other parochial concerns.

But none of this was possible if the leadership did not *start,* at whatever pace was possible and sustainable under the given conditions, to reorganize social relations along lines that promoted such consciousness and attitudes and narrowed the influence of such bourgeois values as personal advancement, along with commodity fetishism, racial and antiwoman prejudice, and national chauvinism. That required strict organization, discipline, and supervision of the work of the trade unions and other mass organizations in carrying out every aspect of economic production, construction, and military defense.

At the same time, in the opening years of the Cuban revolution there was no greater opponent than Che Guevara of what

Lenin referred to as "communist conceit."[27] Guevara placed great emphasis on mastering the skills needed to use the most advanced scientific, production, and financial techniques developed under modern capitalism: cost-accounting methods, financial controls, work organization, and computerization to perform these tasks more effectively. He placed the highest priority on encouraging technical training and advancement of workers. He sought to draw technicians, professionals, and specialists over to the working-class point of view and into the hard work of making production more efficient and cost saving.

Guevara frequently pointed out that Cuba had an advantage over many other oppressed Latin American countries in that some of the U.S.-monopoly-owned enterprises nationalized by the revolutionary government in 1960 had previously instituted systems of accounting and cost controls that were among the most advanced in enterprises anywhere in the world. As a communist, however, Guevara always approached these inheritances from capitalism as a means to a political end; he never allowed the means to determine the ends.

Given the continued existence in a workers' state of social relations and values carried over from the prior capitalist society, Guevara recognized that advanced systems of cost accounting, organization of work, and computerization were not neutral in their consequences when implemented outside the framework of the budgetary finance system. These methods were only advantages for the transition toward socialism if the working class was organized to make *conscious* use of these tools to achieve social and political goals that we have consciously set beforehand. Otherwise, all these mechanisms simply reinforce capitalist methods and "efficiency" as defined by the market.[28]

Guevara put it this way in a talk to a gathering of factory workers in August 1962:

> Building socialism is based on the work of the masses, on the capacities of the masses to be able to organize themselves and to better guide industry, agriculture, and the country's economy. It is based on the capacity of the masses to improve their knowledge every day; on their capacity to incorporate all the technicians, all the compañeros that have remained here to work with us in

the revolution's tasks; on their capacity to create more products for all our people; on their capacity to see the approaching future—approaching in historical terms, not in the life of any one man—and to enter onto the road toward that future with enthusiasm.[29]

That was the objective of the budgetary finance system: *to enter onto the road,* not to prejudge how fast to proceed along it. That would be determined through concrete practical experience in the class struggle. Based on experience in class combat, a study of history, and an understanding of scientific communist theory, Guevara was profoundly convinced that any variant of the economic accounting system—regardless of the intentions of its advocates—not only blocked the working class from entering onto this road, but diverted the toilers onto an opposite course that ultimately threatened the conquests of the workers' state.

According to Rodríguez, during his collaboration with Guevara in the early years of the revolution they had "small differences" on the question of work incentives and methods of payment in factories and other workplaces.

Rodríguez continues: "Our ongoing debate was above all one of proportions: how much weight should be given to moral incentives; how much to material incentives; by how much and in what way can we reduce material incentives to their minimum; and what role can education play in this. The question of the pace of acceleration was where our differences centered."

H ERE TOO, however, there is no evidence that Guevara's course was based on the assumption that it was possible to "hothouse" the transformation of consciousness. His concern was with the political *direction, goals,* and *class consistency* of the policies implemented by the revolutionary government and its communist leadership, and their inevitable results in either advancing or setting back social and internationalist consciousness. "We must make one thing clear," Guevara emphasized in his 1964 article on the budgetary finance system. "*We do not deny the objective need for material [monetary] incentives,* although we are reluctant to use them as the main lever. We believe that in economics this kind of lever quickly takes on an existence of its own and then imposes its strength on the relations among men. It should not be forgotten that it comes from capitalism and is destined to die under socialism"[30] (emphasis in original). Destined to die *under socialism*, Guevara said, not before.

With this political objective in mind, Guevara advocated a system of wage payments and incentives

• that paid workers on the basis of norms pegged first and foremost to their hours worked and the quality of their labor;

• that narrowed differentiation and promoted solidarity among working people by raising the wages and improving the living conditions of the worst-off layers in the factories and fields;

• that shifted the balance of material incentives to the degree possible from purely individual toward collective incentives (e.g., more funds to upgrade housing for the workers in an enterprise, expansion of day-care facilities, construction of cultural and recreational centers, improvements in the commissary, and so on);

• that promoted collective volunteer labor outside the framework of the individual workplace and wages system to build socially useful projects and carry out other social tasks; and

• that encouraged workers to strive to raise their educational and skill level in order to be better able to advance their social responsibilities through their work.

With these considerations in mind, Guevara wrote in his February 1964 article:

> We maintain that in a relatively short time . . . the development of consciousness does more for the development of production than material incentives do. We state this based on the overall development of society toward communism, which presupposes that work will cease to be a tedious necessity and become a pleasant duty.
>
> Being very much a matter of subjective judgment, such a statement requires proof by experience, which is what we are in the middle of doing. If in the course of this experience it were to be demonstrated that our method is a dangerous brake on the development of the productive forces, then we would have to decide to cut our losses

and return to well-trodden paths. Up until now, this has
not happened, and our method, with improvements
through practice, is more and more taking shape and
demonstrating its internal coherence.[31]

As FIDEL CASTRO pointed out in his October 1987 speech, the
leftist mistakes in the late 1960s, following Guevara's departure
from Cuba, were not an application of Che's course. The concrete proposals that Guevara began to implement in enterprises
under the direction of the Ministry of Industry—the work
norms, wage scales, systems of bonuses and penalties, incentives
to skills-upgrading—were gradually dropped and replaced.
Guevara's views on work incentives and norms were thus never
applied in Cuba to the degree Che considered necessary and
possible to accurately test their effectiveness.

Rodríguez remarks that Guevara's proposals on these matters
"are useful in their essence, even though in practice we have
chosen not to apply them." Such a divorce between theory and
practice, however, between ideas and action—between what is
conceded as essential (let alone useful) and what is actually
attempted—is untenable.[32] The mounting social ills in Cuba,
pointed to by Castro and other leaders, that made the rectification process necessary—the privilege, the factory bonuses not
linked to any real advances in output or productivity, the crony-
ism fostered by managers and union functionaries alike, the
waste, the swollen armies of administrative paper shufflers, the
growing absenteeism and demoralization among workers, the
disregard for quality work, the corruption and criminal activities engaged in by significant layers of the Ministry of Interior
and their willingness to attempt to corrupt revolutionists
abroad in the process, the decline of voluntary labor, social
solidarity, and even internationalism: To what are these to be
attributed?

Marxists understand that social relations—and above all social practice, that is, *how we do what we do*—determine the social
being and consciousness of the individual—that is, how *I* do
what *I* do.[33] The fact that for more than fifteen years the Cuban
government and Communist Party "have chosen not to apply"

Guevara's course with regard to incentives and work norms should at least be given serious consideration as one source of the revolution's retreat following implementation of the Economic Management and Planning System.

Fidel Castro explained in his October 1987 speech:

> Che was a realist and did not reject material incentives. He deemed them necessary during the transitional stage, while building socialism. But Che attached more importance—more and more importance—to the conscious factor, to the moral factor.[34]
>
> Che believed in man. And if we don't believe in man, if we think that man is an incorrigible little animal, capable of advancing only if you feed him grass or tempt him with a carrot or hit him with a stick—anybody who believes this, anybody convinced of this will never be a revolutionary; anybody who believes this, anybody convinced of this will never be a socialist; anybody who believes this, anybody convinced of this will never be a communist.[35]

Origins of budgetary finance system

Rodríguez says that the budgetary finance system "appears to us to be a contribution of exceptional value." Guevara did not create this system, Rodríguez continues. "It came from the socialist countries. In the Soviet Union itself for a time, the budgetary finance system regulated many aspects of the economy. But what Che did was work to apply it to a country that was at the same time developing its economy and building socialism."

Rodríguez does not specify what period in the history of the Soviet and Eastern European workers' states he is referring to. But he seems to be alluding to the period of the first several Five-Year Plans under Stalin and his heirs in the Soviet Union (from the late 1920s through the early 1960s), and the initial decade of the Stalinist-led regimes in Eastern Europe, when a system of planning and management sometimes referred to as the budgetary system of financing investment was in use in these countries. Particular organizational aspects of this system bear a formal likeness to elements of the budgetary finance system advocated by Guevara. State enterprises, for example, had no investment funds of their own and were allocated financing from the state budget with no interest charges. By the mid-1960s, the Soviet Union and most Eastern European workers' states had gone over to what was called the economic accounting system, which required state enterprises to rely on their own funds and loans at interest from the state bank.

But it is wrong to trace the lineage of Guevara's proposals to these earlier bureaucratic, anti-working-class systems of planning and management consolidated as part of the Stalinist regimes' violent dispossession of the workers from control over political decision-making and economic planning. Guevara himself claimed no such paternity for the budgetary finance system. (He did, however, explicitly trace the origins of the economic accounting system to the Soviet Union.)[36]

Carlos Tablada is correct in his article in stating that the budgetary finance system "should not be confused, simply because of its name, with budgetary systems that have been utilized previously in sister socialist countries and, later on, in our country." (In its fundamental class orientation as well as various particular aspects, the budgetary finance system *does* share much in common with the Bolsheviks' initial course of economic planning and management by the working class prior to the final stages of "war communism" and the temporary retreat to the New Economic Policy.)[37]

G UEVARA'S COURSE during the opening years of the revolution in Cuba—aimed at increasing the skill levels, participation, mobilization, and control of the producers themselves, and in the process raising their communist consciousness—was the polar opposite of any variant of Stalinist methods. At issue in the discussion on the building of socialism is not choosing between alternative anti-working-class models of planning and management, more or less "efficient," more or less "humane." The choice is not between a system of economic planning and management relying more heavily on a bureaucratic command structure, and an alternative system combining these administrative methods with greater use of capitalist market mechanisms—with both serving the needs of a privileged, petty-bourgeois social layer and reproducing social norms and attitudes that reinforce the caste's domination and drive the toilers further away from political life.

Guevara had no model in this sense and never indicated that he sought to apply one. Instead, he endeavored to use the tools of Marxism, the lessons of communism—especially those learned in practice and written about by Lenin—to help *advance the organization of the toilers* to take growing control over the administration of the state, economy, and society as a whole. This course could have been advanced only in conditions such as those in Cuba (or in the early years of the Soviet Union under Lenin), where a mass revolutionary vanguard of the workers and farmers—not the bureaucratic apparatus of a petty-bourgeois caste—was exercising state power. Whatever its errors, whatever the gaps in its communist education and experience, that mass revolutionary leadership in Cuba was consciously seeking to organize the workers and farmers to advance toward socialism, and continues to do so to this day.[38]

Guevara did seek to learn from experience—both in Cuba and the experience of other workers' states. In fact, in his capacity as a leader of Cuba's revolutionary government and Communist Party, Guevara visited the Soviet Union and Eastern Europe numerous times and wrote down his critical observations. More than twenty-five years before the deep public crisis in the Soviet Union and collapse of Stalinist parties throughout Eastern Europe, Guevara pointed to the political and economic policies of these regimes that he believed to be barriers to the building of socialism and development of communist consciousness. Most of these writings have either never been published or are long out of print in editions that even at the time had very small press runs.

ONE OF GUEVARA'S observations about the political consequences of the system of economic planning and management in the USSR and Eastern Europe is cited by Cuban author Fernando Martínez in his book *Che: El socialismo y el comunismo* (Che: socialism and communism), which was awarded the 1989 Casa de las Américas Special Prize by the Havana-based cultural institute. When the economic accounting system in these countries "comes, as it must, to a dead end," Guevara wrote, "it is led by its own logic to try to overcome this by again resorting to the same system—that is, to increase material incentives and to increasingly focus people's attention on their own material interests. This leads eventually to free rein for the law of value and ultimately to the resurgence, in a certain sense, of strictly capitalist categories."[39]

This can be read as astounding prophecy by Guevara about the denouement that would unfold in Eastern Europe and the Soviet Union in the 1980s and early 1990s. But it was not prophecy. Instead, as Guevara said, he was simply pointing to the irreversible logic of the economic accounting system. Guevara was a revolutionary scientist, not a secular prophet, crank, or idiot savant.

New Economic Policy
In this regard, it is also useful to look at Guevara's assessment of the New Economic Policy instituted in 1921 in the Soviet republic under the revolutionary leadership of Lenin and the Bolsheviks.

Faced with the devastation of industry, agricultural production, trade, and social life caused by several years of capitalist- and landlord-backed civil war and imperialist invasions, the Soviet government and Communist Party adopted policies that (1) expanded market relations in the exchange of agricultural commodities and industrial goods between peasants in the countryside and workers in the cities; and (2) introduced greater self-financing and profit criteria into the operations of reviving Soviet industries.

The policies of "war communism" followed by the Soviet government from mid-1918 through early 1921 as necessary measures of defense and survival were no longer sustainable with the end of the fighting. Under civil war conditions, the revolutionary government had relied on growing militarization of labor in the factories and transportation, as well as on compulsory requisitions of the peasants' grain surpluses to feed the urban working class and Red Army. The grain requisitioning had been at least tolerable to broad layers of peasants so long as they saw it as a temporary measure, one that was necessary to the military effort to prevent reimposition of rule by brutal counterrevolutionary landlords. (Even so, there were many forms of peasant resistance to forced requisitions throughout the war.)

With the defeat of the counterrevolution, however, sporadic resistance turned into open revolt by peasants, especially in the face of widespread famine in many regions. Peasants often refused to plant; they slaughtered their livestock rather than have their surplus production confiscated by the state. The peasants aspired to restore at least the rudiments of what they considered normal life—enough food to eat, some tools and seed to work the land, a roof over their heads, clothes on their backs, and some produce to sell on the market.

At the same time, the marshaling of industry and transportation to meet pressing war needs had called for methods of management organized along the lines of the military command structures of the Red Army. The distribution of industrial goods was subordinated to the war effort, drastically reducing supplies of needed tools for the peasantry and consumer items for both peasants and urban workers. The mobilization of labor was often organized along lines of military conscription and discipline as well. But with the end of the civil war, measures had to be taken to reverse the virtual collapse of the production and circulation of manufactured goods, to restore industry, to rebuild the trade unions as the industrial working class increased in size, and to revive supplies of tools and consumer goods to the countryside in exchange for needed farm products to the cities.

At the 1921 congress of the soviets in Russia, Lenin explained the objective situation that made the NEP necessary for the survival of the worker-peasant alliance on which the very existence of the revolutionary government and the stability of the proletarian Communist Party were based:

> When there is no flourishing large-scale industry which can be organised in such a way as to supply the peasants with goods immediately, then the gradual development of a powerful alliance of workers and peasants is possible only through trade and the gradual advance of agriculture and industry above their present level, under the guidance and control of the workers' state. Sheer necessity has driven us to this path. And this is the sole basis

and substance of our New Economic Policy. . . .

That is why we have unanimously declared that we shall carry out this policy in earnest and for a long time, but, of course, as has already been correctly noted, not forever; it has been made necessary by our poverty and devastation and by the tremendous weakening of our large-scale industry.[40]

LENIN, TROTSKY, and other Bolshevik leaders explicitly and publicly referred to the NEP as a temporary but necessary "retreat" from the revolution's course toward expanding socialist relations of production and interchange.[41] Reknitting the alliance between the workers and peasants was a precondition for renewing that advance.

The Bolsheviks were very much aware of the dangers of increased class differentiation and polarization inevitably bred by the NEP. These policies widened social inequalities and helped generate new exploiting layers, especially rich peasants and price-gouging traders and middlemen (whom the workers and poor peasants came to call "Nepmen," with contempt). State industrial enterprises, pressed to cut costs, laid off workers and pushed up jobless levels in the cities. Making the profit column of the ledger look good became the overriding consideration for many factory managers—whether or not these figures reflected less wasteful organization of labor and utilization of resources, and regardless of broader social needs and priorities. Efforts to advance workers' control as well as steps toward workers' management had to overcome more obstacles in the factories.

To combat such consequences of the NEP, the Bolsheviks worked to rebuild the strength of the Communist Party among the reviving industrial working class and to fight for political leadership of the peasantry, especially the big majority of non-exploiting peasants who hired no labor and rented out no livestock or equipment.

At the eleventh Communist Party congress in March 1922, Lenin warned that "the fight against capitalist society has become a hundred times more fierce and perilous, because we are not always able to tell enemies from friends. . . . That is why attention must be concentrated mainly on the question: 'Who will win?'"—The proletariat? Or the newly emerging capitalist layers?[42]

The "state is in our hands," Lenin continued, "but has it operated the New Economic Policy in the way we wanted in this past year? No. . . . The machine refused to obey the hand that guided it. It was like a car that was going not in the direction the driver desired, but in the direction someone else desired; as if it were being driven by some mysterious, lawless hand, God knows whose, perhaps of a profiteer, or of a private capitalist, or of both."[43]

In face of this demonstration of the consequences of the inexorable workings of the law of value, Lenin proposed a shift in course to more effectively mobilize the working class to combat the negative consequences of the NEP. "For a year we have been retreating," he said at the 1922 party congress. "On behalf of the Party we must now call a halt. The purpose pursued by the retreat has been achieved. This period is drawing, or has drawn, to a close. We now have a different objective, that of regrouping our forces."[44]

The Bolsheviks' proposal to halt the retreat did not yet mean turning away from the NEP itself, which, as Lenin put it a few months later, "remains the main, current, and all-embracing slogan of today."[45] Instead, the Bolsheviks aimed at drawing the broad mass of small peasant commodity-producers toward the socialist course of the proletarian state, while steps were taken, to the degree resources permitted, to rebuild heavy industry (and thus strengthen the industrial working class) and increasingly restrict the operation of capitalist prices of production in the functioning of manufacturing, wholesale trade, and freight transportation.

CENTRAL TO THIS perspective was Lenin's proposal in January 1923 to promote the voluntary organization of peasants and other independent commodity producers into state-sponsored cooperatives that would (1) sell manufactured goods in the villages, (2) process and market the peasants' produce, and (3) provide needed credit at low interest rates.

"We went too far when we introduced NEP," Lenin wrote, "but not because we attached too much importance to the principle of free enterprise and trade—we went too far because we lost sight of the cooperatives. . . .

"Indeed," Lenin said, "the power of the state over all large-scale means of production, political power in the hands of the proletariat, the alliance of this proletariat with the many millions of small and very small peasants, the assured proletarian leadership of the peasantry, etc.—is this not all that is necessary to build a complete socialist society out of co-operatives? . . . It is still not the building of socialist society, but it is all that is necessary and sufficient for it."[46]

These proposals by Lenin were not new in their fundamentals; they pointed toward returning, to the degree possible, to the course the Bolsheviks had organized the working class and peasantry to carry out in the opening years of the Soviet republic, before the civil war and its consequences forced a retreat. Some three years prior to his 1922 articles on cooperatives, Lenin summarized the initial course of the workers' and peasants' government in an October 1919 article entitled, "Economics and Politics in the Era of the Dictatorship of the Proletariat."

> We speak of the "the first steps" of communism in Russia . . . because all these things have been only partially effected in our country, or, to put it differently, their achievement is only in its early stages. We accomplished instantly, at one revolutionary blow, all that can, in general, be accomplished instantly; on the first day of the dictatorship of the proletariat, for instance, on October 26 (November 8), 1917, the private ownership of land was abolished without compensation for the big landowners—the big landowners were expropriated. Within the space of a few months practically all the big capitalists, owners of factories, joint-stock companies, banks, railways, and so forth, were also expropriated without compensation.
>
> The state organisation of large-scale production in industry and the transition from "workers' control" to "workers' management" of factories and railways—this

has, by and large, already been accomplished; but in relation to agriculture it has only just begun ("state farms," i.e., large farms organised by the workers' state on state-owned land). Similarly, we have only just begun the organisation of various forms of co-operative societies of small farmers as a transition from petty commodity agriculture to socialist agriculture.

The same must be said of the state-organised distribution of products in place of private trade, i.e., the state procurement and delivery of grain to the cities and of industrial products to the countryside.[47]

The political fight launched by Lenin during the last year of his active political life, aimed among other things at combating the dangerous initial consequences of the NEP and reversing the Soviet republic's unavoidable temporary retreat, was one of his final contributions to Marxism and working-class politics.[48]

Above all, the NEP had assumed the existence in the Soviet Union of a communist leadership of the working class that worked to strengthen the worker-peasant alliance, increase the production and circulation of food and other agricultural goods, and revive industrial production as rapidly as possible, in order to lay a more solid foundation on which to organize the next steps in advancing toward socialist relations of production and interchange.

Thus, to simply assert, as Rodríguez does, that the "New Economic Policy was based fundamentally on the economic accounting system" is to miss the specific situation confronting Lenin and the Bolsheviks in the early 1920s. The NEP was a *temporary retreat* organized to make it possible for the Bolsheviks to regroup the vanguard of the working class and strengthen its leadership of the toiling peasants. On the basis of that worker-peasant alliance, it would be possible to organize a *detour* toward reviving the level of the productive forces in the Soviet republics to the point where the offensive could be retaken in advancing large-scale, conscious socialist planning to determine economic and social priorities. By applying the NEP as a temporary retreat, Lenin and the Bolsheviks were seeking to get the Soviet workers' state back to a level of production and exchange that would allow them to advance the same socialist objectives as those advocated by Guevara some four decades later under substantially more favorable objective conditions.

As SUMMARIZED BY Rodríguez, Guevara "after a careful analysis of Lenin's writings . . . concluded that the NEP was more a tactical than a strategic conception." Guevara's assessment of the NEP and its lessons is consistent with Lenin's evaluation of the NEP.

In Guevara's February 1964 article on the budgetary finance system, he wrote that "the economic and political situation in the Soviet Union made necessary the retreat Lenin spoke of. The entire policy, therefore, can be characterized as a tactic closely linked to the country's historical situation."[49] Thus, Guevara explained, supporters of the economic accounting system in Cuba and elsewhere were wrong in attempting to point to the NEP as a strategic course to build socialism. The policies that made up the NEP could not be accorded universal validity if abstracted from the level of industrialization, state of agricultural production, firmness of the worker-farmer alliance, the presence or absence of the consequences of civil war, and retreat in the international class struggle.

Lenin and the Bolsheviks were firmly convinced that deepening the course toward socialism in the Soviet Union was completely intertwined with the advance of the international struggle for national liberation and socialism. It was Stalin who introduced the anti-internationalist perspective of "socialism in one country" following Lenin's death.

Similarly, Guevara's decision in 1965 to take up internationalist missions first in Africa and then Bolivia was consistent with his political course inside Cuba to advance the construction of socialism. Guevara recognized that a worker and peasant victory elsewhere in Latin America—where social and political conditions were ripening for revolutionary explosions—would accomplish more than anything else in opening the road to further advances toward building socialism in Cuba itself.

Guevara wrote his final major statement on the issues under debate in Cuba in early 1965, just prior to departing for the internationalist missions in the Congo and Bolivia. That article,

"Socialism and Man in Cuba," was first published in March 1965 in Uruguay, the month that Guevara dropped from public view in Cuba; and it first appeared in print in Cuba the following month, when Guevara left the island.

I F A COMMUNIST'S "revolutionary zeal is blunted when the most urgent tasks have been accomplished on a local scale and he forgets about proletarian internationalism," Guevara wrote in the 1965 article, "the revolution he leads will cease to be a driving force and sink into a comfortable drowsiness that imperialism, our irreconcilable enemy, will utilize to gain ground. Proletarian internationalism is a duty, but it is also a revolutionary necessity. This is the way we educate our people."[50]

Finally, it should be noted that Cuba's communist leadership has greater achievements to its credit in forging and maintaining a worker-farmer alliance than any since the time of Lenin and the Bolsheviks. It carried out a thoroughgoing agrarian reform in the first years of the revolution, providing land and the wherewithal to till it to working farmers and establishing an extensive network of state farms producing sugar, livestock, and various crops. Especially since 1977 the Cuban government has made substantial progress in organizing farmers on a voluntary basis to establish cooperatives, which have contributed both toward raising the productivity of agricultural labor and improving the living and working conditions of the rural producers.[51]

The adoption of the Economic Management and Planning System and the market-based principles underlying it posed a serious threat to this worker-peasant alliance, and to further advances in agricultural production as well. As part of the rectification process, for example, the Cuban government in 1986 shut down the so-called free farmers' market that had been established in 1980 and had led to growing profiteering on food products by layers of farmers and middlemen in Cuba. As Fidel Castro has explained, spiraling food prices were putting the alliance of farmers and urban workers under mounting strains, while the course toward expanding voluntary organization of cooperatives was seriously undermined by the quick and easy profits to be gained by individual farmers on unregulated markets. Illegal renting of farmland began to appear in the country-side. Crop theft and diversion of state- or cooperative-owned building supplies, transportation equipment, and farm machinery for private use was accelerated. Some cooperatives scaled back production of food and turned to producing brooms and other commodities to be sold at the unregulated farmers' markets.

In the May 1987 *L'Humanité* interview previously cited, Castro linked the decision to shut down the so-called farmers' market to the broader need to rectify the consequences of the course undertaken in Cuba with the creation of "a system of management and planning, copying the experience of the socialist countries." The farmers' market, Castro said, "should never have been established. It was an error."[52]

Economic planning

Rodríguez writes that Guevara had "a very clear conception of the role of planning as a permanent instrument of the economy."

Actually, however, Guevara had a much more comprehensive understanding of the place of centralized planning during the transition to socialism than simply an "instrument of the economy." Guevara wrote:

> The law of value and the plan are two terms linked by a contradiction and its resolution. We can therefore state that centralized planning is the mode of existence of socialist society, its defining characteristic, and the point at which man's consciousness finally succeeds in synthesizing and directing the economy toward its goal: the full liberation of the human being within the framework of communist society.[53]

Rodríguez acknowledges that "the plan is contradictory to utilizing the market and, consequently, to utilizing the law of value." But Rodríguez adds:

> The plan becomes more reconcilable with utilizing the market and the law of value when the law of value is interpreted as partially operative—that is, when we utilize it rather than allowing it to conquer us. An example of this

was when we established the market as an element
steered by the country's economic leadership bodies.

In the article "On the Concept of Value" reprinted in this
issue, Guevara responded to a similar point made by Alberto
Mora some twenty-five years earlier. "Under socialism," Mora
had stated, "the law of value operates through the plan."
Guevara replied:

> We are not so sure.
> Let us suppose a plan is drafted in which all categories
> are in complete harmony. To evaluate this plan, one
> would have to suppose the existence of some instrument
> of analysis outside the plan itself. As far as I can see, this
> instrument of analysis could only be the results of the
> plan. But such results are the verification after the fact
> that all went well or that something went badly (with re-
> spect to the law of value, that is; there could also be de-
> fects of other origin). . . .
> Let us suppose something closer to reality. Let us sup-
> pose that measures need to be taken in response to a
> given situation—for example, spending on defense, to
> correct big imbalances in domestic production, on invest-
> ments that eat up part of our capacity to produce con-
> sumer goods but are necessary because of their strategic
> importance (I refer here to economic as well as military
> considerations). Tensions will be created that will have to
> be remedied by administrative measures to prevent a sud-
> den jump in prices. This in turn will create new relations
> that will increasingly obscure the operation of the law of
> value.
> The effects can always be calculated. The capitalists do
> it in their studies of cyclical trends. But the law of value
> will be less and less reflected in the plan. This is our view
> on the subject.

So, for Guevara, the plan was not an "instrument of the
economy" wielded by a planning body standing *outside* the plan.
It was not a matrix of production quotas and distribution ratios
drawn up by proficient technocrats to administer the economy—or, more precisely, to administer the organization of the

social labor of workers and working farmers who produce society's wealth.

Instead, for guevara the plan was the totality of the ways during the transition to socialism that the working class takes growing, conscious control over the priorities, organization, and administration of economic and social life. The working class and its political vanguard (including those engaged in necessary administrative tasks in factories, state farms, or other economic, social, and political institutions) operate *within* the plan.

What *does* stand outside the plan during the transition to socialism, Guevara says, are its results, which serve the working class as an "instrument of analysis" to judge how well or how badly they are doing in advancing consciously determined goals and priorities. As already discussed, the more the working class expands its conscious control over economic and social priorities and administration, the more restricted and limited becomes the weight of the blind laws of the market—which, like the bureaucracy, also stands outside the plan and in antagonism to it.

Guevara's extensive writings on this subject do not support the view expressed by Rodríguez that the "plan becomes more reconcilable with utilizing the market and the law of value when the law of value is interpreted as partially operative—that is, when we utilize it rather than allowing it to conquer us." The problem is not one of "interpreting" the law of value as "partially operative" during the transition. It *is* partially operative— so long as new, socialist relations of production have not been established and consolidated on a world scale. But, as Guevara pointed out in his response to Mora, as the toilers expand their control over economic decision-making, "the law of value will be less and less reflected in the plan." The law of value, together with the markets through which it operates, will not be steered more firmly; they will wither away.

Guevara's view of the plan in the transition to socialism is especially important in light of the economic and social dead end into which the Soviet Union and Eastern European workers' states were driven by the privileged castes in those countries. There is nothing inherently efficient or productive—let alone proletarian or socialist—about a system of economic planning administered by a petty-bourgeois social layer with interests alien to those of the workers and farmers.

To the contrary, these are bourgeois planning methods. They do not advance society toward socialism, that is, along the historic line of march of the working class. Such planning—carried out on the property foundations of the expropriation of the bourgeoisie by the working class—can produce rapid growth for a period of time in a relatively economically backward society with a large peasantry and a small industrial working class. The Stalinist regime that consolidated its stranglehold over the Soviet toilers industrialized the USSR in the 1930s, '40s, and '50s by transferring surplus labor power from the countryside to work in factories and urban construction; by opening vast new regions to cultivation, mining, and forestry; by initially reaping the benefits of large increases in economies of scale; by emulating or utilizing technology already developed in industrially advanced capitalist countries (and already heading toward obsolescence); and by holding down the living standards and intensifying the labor of the toilers.

THE CUMULATIVE results of these Stalinist methods of bureaucratic planning, however, destroyed rather than encouraged initiative by working people in the cities and in the countryside and undermined communist attitudes toward work. Not only will the degenerated Soviet workers' state and other such regimes never catch up with the most industrially advanced capitalist countries in labor productivity and living standards, they will continue to fall further behind.

There is no way to reorganize labor, modernize production in industry and agriculture, and produce goods of high and increasing quality without deepening communist consciousness, expanding workers' control and management, strengthening the worker-peasant alliance, and broadening workers' democracy in the government as a whole. That is the only way for the toilers to advance toward socialism, and that was what the budgetary finance system that Guevara sought to organize the working class to implement was designed to aid.

It is common among those who admire Guevara's personal example and his political contributions to point to the breadth of his "interests"—ranging from the most complex questions of economics and politics to the details of enterprise management and financial accounting; from the art of revolutionary warfare to regular collaboration with workers to advance their organization in the factories, other workplaces, study institutes, and the armed forces. This view of Guevara misses the point, however. For Guevara, there was no separation between these aspects of his practical activity as a leader of the Cuban revolution and the communist workers' movement.

Guevara acted on the scientific and political conviction that communism was not a set of good ideas or prescriptions to improve society. He was not interested in social engineering, in developing planning bureaus staffed by growing numbers of technocrats and administrators, no matter how well meaning. Guevara's political course was guided by the understanding, as Frederick Engels explained more than 140 years ago, that "communism is not a doctrine but a *movement;* it proceeds not from principles but from *facts. . . .* Communism, insofar as it is a theory, is the theoretical expression of the position of the proletariat in [the class] struggle and the theoretical summation of the conditions for the liberation of the proletariat."[54]

Either the working class would be organized by its communist vanguard to transform social relations *through the plan,* and in the process transform themselves, Guevara was convinced, or there would be no progress toward socialism.

Thus, Guevara's rejection of Mora's assertion that "the law of value operates through the plan" helps us understand why anything that stands outside the plan, and *uses* it, can only be a bureaucracy—not the working class and its political vanguard, which function *within* and *through* the plan. No state or party institution can "steer the market" (the experience with the "free farmers' market" in Cuba confirms the results of such an illusion). No matter how revolutionary the intentions of the leadership, the market will assert its own laws that increasingly "steer" the evolution of social relations toward capitalism and away from socialism. What Guevara explained in his answer to Mora reinforces the reality that working-class centralization through planning is the *opposite* of the growth of bureaucracy, where bureaus and their privileged cadres—not workers and their committees—are the planners.

Budgetary finance system: an integrated whole

In advancing the building of socialism in Cuba, the obstacles that have been targeted by the rectification process cannot be overcome, as Carlos Tablada puts it in his article, "simply by indiscriminately grafting elements" of Guevara's budgetary finance system onto the economic accounting system. Tablada advances the judgment that "the system of managing the economy that arises out of the rectification process—whatever name it may be given, will stem not from the economic accounting system but rather from the thought of Che and Fidel."

Guevara himself emphasized that the budgetary finance system "is a comprehensive concept. That is, its objective operation would take effect when applied to all areas of the economy, in a single whole. . . ."[55]

Rodríguez expresses a different viewpoint on this matter, as well. "Among the ideas on the budgetary finance system of economic management postulated by Che are some extremely timely ideas for what we are doing today," he writes. "And with regard to the economic accounting system—the system we use today, the one Che was so critical of—I would say that if we do not put many of Che's ideas into practice, then we will not be able to move forward. A symbiosis is necessary."

Rodríguez singles out Guevara's insistence on rigorous cost accounting; his approach to job categories and wage scales; his emphasis on quality as well as quantity in work norms; the elements of socialist morality and communist consciousness he embodied; and a number of other policy proposals.

But these individual elements ultimately mean little when severed from the budgetary finance system and the overall political course advanced by Guevara. For Guevara, building socialism is the conscious organization of the production and distribution of goods and services by the working class so as to advance the self-transformation of working people into new human beings, into socialist men and women, as they transform their economic and social relations and their conditions of life and work.

The events in the Soviet Union and Eastern Europe over the past several years—and the developments in Cuba itself that continue to make rectification necessary—point to the problem with Rodríguez's assessment that communists in Cuba today must "accept the deficiencies and shortcomings that stem from the economic accounting system." This is the case, he argues, since "the budgetary finance system demands conditions and possibilities we cannot attain, either in the medium term or even in the more distant future.... It is based on forms of economic controls that are closer to communism.... It is a leap like the one proposed by Karl Marx, from capitalism to an advanced socialism. As everyone knows, we have not made that leap. Not even the Soviet Union has done so."

M ARX, HOWEVER, never "proposed a leap . . . from capitalism to an advanced socialism." He proposed the use of state power by the working class to expropriate big capital, establish the dictatorship of the proletariat, and on that basis begin reorganizing economic and social relations as part of advancing the worldwide struggle for socialism. During that transitional period (Marx never claimed to know beforehand its duration or the details of its development), the laws of motion, class institutions, and methods carried over from the prior capitalist society gradually wither away and are replaced by new forms of human relations and social organization.

Rodríguez's statement that "not even the Soviet Union" has yet completed that leap from capitalism to advanced socialism could be seen to imply that the simple industrial development and material progress of a workers' state is a gauge of that society's advance toward socialism. Despite the emergence of the Soviet Union as an industrial power over the past sixty years, however, its course ever since the consolidation of the petty-bourgeois caste under Stalin at the close of the 1920s has been away from socialism, not toward it.[56]

Most importantly, it is impossible for the working class anywhere in the world, including in Cuba, to make progress in advancing toward socialism on the basis of a "symbiosis" of the budgetary finance system and a variant of bureaucratic planning methods, which is what the economic accounting system is. The twentieth century has produced no alternative to the communist course advocated by Guevara as to how a revolutionary workers' leadership must organize economic planning and management in a workers' state.

The economic accounting system is not a less adequate but more practical road toward building socialism than that advocated by Guevara. *It is not a road toward socialism at all.* It becomes a way for privileged social layers in the state and party apparatus to block the advance of the working class toward becoming the masters of society. The proof is now in, from Bulgaria to Siberia: the economic accounting system disorganizes production and undermines social progress and human culture.

The communist road is not immediately open to the toilers of every country in today's world, regardless of that country's level of economic and social development (for example, the case of Burkina Faso cited earlier). The specific forms and methods employed to advance along this road will vary depending on concrete economic and social conditions, the strength and revolutionary experience of the working class, and other factors. Revolutionary leadership may need, more than once, to organize a temporary retreat in the face of objective conditions, as was done in the Soviet Union under Lenin's leadership during the period of the New Economic Policy.

B UT THERE IS no alternative road to socialism. Just as it's not possible to transform a bureaucratized trade union into a class-struggle instrument by adopting militant rhetoric or cosmetic reforms to make it appear more democratic; just as it's not possible to reform a social democratic or Stalinist party by getting it to adopt a few revolutionary-sounding positions— even less so is it possible to transform the economic accounting system by garnishing it with a basket of particular policies borrowed from Che Guevara and the budgetary finance system.

To the contrary, in order to continue to advance, Cuban communists will confront the necessity of doing what Fidel Castro correctly insists has yet to be tried in Cuba: *a serious attempt to put Guevara's proposals into practice.*

Such an effort to enter back onto the communist road not followed since the opening years of the Soviet Union under Lenin's leadership has not yet been posed by even a small political vanguard in any workers' state other than Cuba. The fact that a serious discussion of Guevara's course is under way in Cuba as part of rectification is a tribute not only to the central leadership cadre of the government and Communist Party, but above all to the internationalism, political commitment, and revolutionary consciousness of broad layers of workers, farmers, soldiers, and youth in that country. In their hands, together with those of revolutionists of action like them the world over, lies the possibility of socialist revolution and the communist construction of socialism and its new men and women.

The Changing Face of U.S. Politics

Working Class Politics and the Trade Unions
by Jack Barnes

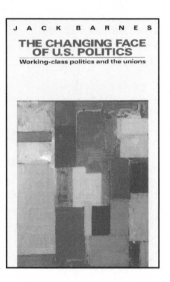

A handbook for workers coming into the factories, mines, and mills, as they react to the uncertainty, turmoil, and brutality of capitalism in the closing years of the twentieth century.
It shows how millions of workers, as political resistance grows, will revolutionize themselves, their unions, and all of society.
$19.95

"The ultimate contradiction facing American imperialism is that it must be able to intervene militarily around the world or else capitalism will be overthrown piecemeal. But to do so, the rulers have to take on the American working class, which more and more sees that it has no stake in Washington's military adventures abroad. And this contradiction is the most decisive in world politics."

FROM PATHFINDER. SEE ADDRESSES ON PAGE 2

Nelson Mandela Speaks

Forging a Democratic, Nonracial South Africa

Mandela's speeches from 1990 through 1993 recount the course of struggle that put an end to apartheid and opened the fight for a deep-going political, economic, and social transformation in South Africa. $18.95

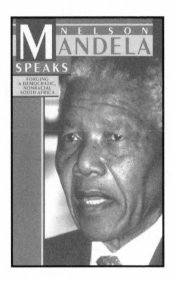

Thomas Sankara Speaks

The Burkina Faso Revolution 1983–87

Speeches and writings by the assassinated president of Burkina Faso tell the story of the revolution that unfolded in this West African country. Internationalism and support for the struggles of peasants, workers, and women were hallmarks of Sankara's revolutionary leadership. 260 pp., $18.95

Women's Liberation and the African Freedom Struggle

by Thomas Sankara

Explains the origins of women's oppression and the struggle needed to end it, with special attention to women in Africa. 36 pp., $3.00

TWO ARTICLES BY
ERNESTO CHE GUEVARA

"Building socialism is based on the capacities of the masses to organize themselves and to better guide industry, agriculture, and the country's economy." Che Guevara, August 1962.

ON THE CONCEPT OF VALUE

A reply to Alberto Mora

by Ernesto Che Guevara

I N THIS ISSUE of *Nuestra Industria, Revista Económica,* we are reprinting an article by Alberto Mora.[1] The article, entitled "On the Functioning of the Law of Value in the Cuban Economy Today," recently appeared in *Comercio Exterior,* the journal of the Ministry of Foreign Trade.[2]

The article begins by stating: "Some comrades contend that the law of value no longer functions within the state sector of the Cuban economy." Refuting arguments is important, but identifying those who hold the viewpoint being challenged is also important. "Some comrades" have neither first names nor last names. But the individuals to whom the critique is directed do. They are the minister of industry, who is the author of this article, and Comrade Luis Alvarez Rom, the minister of finance—not to mention others who, as part of the current supporting the budgetary finance system, may also be intended as targets of criticism.

We say this at the outset, since it is a good idea to identify not only concepts but also the persons who hold them.

We would like to take up three points Mora makes in his conclusions. In our opinion, the most important point in the article is not its dispute with those who reject the operation of the law of value in the state sector. The most important question is how Mora defines value itself, which does not correspond with Marx's views.

This article appeared in the October 1963 issue of Nuestra Industria, Revista Económica, *a publication of the Ministry of Industry. Guevara headed this ministry for four years following its establishment in February 1961.*

ENDNOTES FOR THIS ARTICLE BEGIN ON PAGE 199.

Mora states:

> What is value? In my opinion, if we are to give consistent meaning to the category of value, we must keep in mind that value embodies (or more accurately, expresses) a relation. It is, first of all, a measurement, and as such expresses a relation. Second, and consequently, value is a category created by man under specific circumstances and with a specific purpose in mind. It is thus part and parcel of the social relations man develops.

Let us take a closer look at this paragraph.

A few lines earlier, referring to value, Mora says: "But the measurement of something is not the same as the thing itself." Now he is saying that value "is, first of all, a measurement, and as such expresses a relation." This strikes us as a contradiction.

He then says: "Second, and consequently, value is a category created by man under specific circumstances and with a specific purpose in mind."

This is in complete contradiction with the views expressed by Marx on the economic laws of society. Marx's work was devoted to laying bare the essence of phenomena beneath their appearance. He sought to show how the various fetishes acquired by humanity serve only to conceal its ignorance.

IN OUR VIEW, if there is one thing human beings have not been able to do, it is to create value for a specific purpose. The relations of production gave rise to value. Value exists objectively, whether or not we are aware of its existence. Our knowledge or lack of knowledge has no bearing on the existence of value. Nor does it have any bearing on the spontaneous way in which capitalist relations of production express themselves.

Beginning with Marx, much light has been shed on the intricate mechanisms of capitalist relations of production. This knowledge, however, does not alter reality. Human beings can change society under certain conditions, but they cannot "invent" its laws.

Further on, Mora adds: "Remember that only one type of labor creates value: socially necessary labor, that is, labor that applies limited available resources to satisfy a socially recognized need. It is precisely this relation that is expressed in the category of value. In other words, this relation is, properly speaking, value."

We should note that Mora gives the phrase "socially necessary" a content different from its actual meaning. He uses it simply to denote that something is "necessary to society." But "socially necessary" actually refers to a measurement of the amount of labor that society as a whole must perform to produce a value. Mora concludes by stating that value is the relation between needs and resources.

It is clear that if society sees no usefulness in a product, then the item will have no exchange-value. (This is perhaps the source of Mora's conceptual error in the way he views socially necessary labor.) But it is no less clear that Marx identifies the notion of value with abstract labor. The search for a way to measure labor is directly related to the search for a measurement of value. In *Capital* we read the following:

> A use-value, or useful article, therefore, has value only because abstract human labour is objectified or materialized in it. How, then, is the magnitude of this value to be measured? By means of the quantity of the "value-forming substance," the labour, contained in the article.[3]

The point is that there can be no value without use-value. At the same time, it is impossible to conceive of use-value without value (with the exception of certain forces of nature), because of the dialectical relationship between the two.

It would be closer to reality to say that the relationship between needs and resources is implicit in the concept of value. That seems logical enough since this formula is interchangeable with the relationship between supply and demand—a relationship that exists in the market, where it forms one of the links in the operation of the law of value or value relations.

So this is our first objection. The point is important because of the danger that would result from treating the question of value so schematically that it is reduced to a simple restatement of the law of supply and demand.

Turning to the first paragraph of Mora's article, we would say that the assessment found there is not correct. We look at the question of value in a different light. I refer back to our article published in *Nuestra Industria, Revista Económica,* no. 1, which states:

> When all products have prices with a relationship among themselves distinct from the relationship among these products on the capitalist market, then we will have created a new price structure with no parallel on the world market. How do we then ensure that these prices coincide with value? How can we consciously use our knowledge of the law of value to attain market equilibrium on the one hand, and prices that faithfully reflect real costs on the other? This is one of the most serious problems faced by the socialist economy.[4]

In other words, no one questions that the law of value continues to operate. What we are saying is that this law operates in its most developed form through the capitalist market. And as a consequence, modifications introduced into the market by social ownership of the means of production and the distribution apparatus bring about changes that make it difficult to assess how the law operates.

We view the law of value as the regulator of commodity relations under capitalism. Therefore, to the extent the market is distorted for whatever reason, certain distortions will also occur in the operation of the law of value.

The form and degree to which this happens have not been studied with the same depth as that with which Marx conducted his study of capitalism. Marx and Engels did not foresee that the transition period might begin in economically backward countries and thus did not devote much study or attention to the economic characteristics of such a situation.

Lenin, for all his genius, did not have the time to make a detailed study—Marx had an entire lifetime for such studies—of the economic problems of a transitional stage of this kind, which combines two elements: the historical fact of a society emerging from capitalism without having completed the stage of capitalist development (and in which remnants of feudalism still survive); and the transfer of the ownership of the means of production into the hands of the people.

The possibility of such a situation was foreseen by Lenin in his study of the uneven development of capitalism, the emergence of imperialism, and his theory of the imperialist system breaking at its weakest link at times of social upheavals such as wars.[5] With the Russian revolution and the creation of the first socialist state, Lenin proved the feasibility of such an occurrence. He did not have time to pursue his investigation, however, since he devoted himself in full to consolidating power and participating in the revolution—as he announced in the abrupt ending to his book *The State and Revolution.*[6] (The whole of Lenin's writings on the economy of the transition period serve as an extremely valuable introduction to the topic, although they lack the development and thoroughness that time and experience would have given them.)

In his conclusions, Comrade Mora states categorically:

> Under socialism the law of value continues operating, although it is not the only criterion regulating production. Under socialism the law of value operates through the plan.

We are not so sure.

Let us suppose a plan is drafted in which all categories are in complete harmony. To evaluate this plan, one would have to suppose the existence of some instrument of analysis outside the plan itself. As far as I can see, this instrument of analysis could only be the results of the plan. But such results are the verification after the fact that all went well or that something went badly (with respect to the law of value, that is; there could also be defects of other origin).

WE WOULD THEN have to begin a detailed study of the weak points of the plan to try to take practical measures—once again after the fact—to correct the situation by successive approximations. In any case, the equilibrium between supply and effective demand would be the determining factor.[7] Analysis of unsatisfied needs would shed no further light since, by definition, conditions do not exist for providing man with all that he wants during this period.

Let us suppose something closer to reality. Let us suppose that measures need to be taken in response to a given situation—for example, spending on defense, to correct big imbalances in domestic production, on investments that eat up part of our capacity to produce consumer goods but are necessary because of their strategic importance (I refer here to economic as well as military considerations). Tensions will be created that will have to be remedied by administrative measures to prevent a sudden jump in prices. This in turn will create new relations that will increasingly obscure the operation of the law of value.

The effects can always be calculated. The capitalists do it in their studies of cyclical trends. But the law of value will be less and less reflected in the plan. This is our view on the subject.

We would also like to take up another part of the article, where Mora states:

> When some comrades contend that the law of value no longer functions within the state sector of the Cuban economy, they are arguing that the entire state sector is under single ownership, that the enterprises are the property of society. This is of course true. But from an economic point of view, it is the wrong criterion. State property is not yet fully developed social property. That will only come with communism.

And later:

> It is enough simply to look at relations between state enterprises—how contradictions emerge between them, how some complain about others—to realize that in Cuba today the state sector as a whole in no way constitutes a single large enterprise.

Mora is referring either to a conversation we had, to remarks I made at the end of the term at the School of Administration, or to an unpublished pamphlet by Comrade Alvarez Rom, where this goal is referred to as one of Lenin's aspirations. The pamphlet discusses treating factories as departments of a consolidated enterprise and expresses the aspiration—to the degree the development of the economy permits—of raising all relations to the level that would exist in a single big factory.

It is true that contradictions exist between enterprises—and I am not speaking of enterprises in the economy in general, but of those under the Ministry of Industry. But it is no less true that contradictions exist between the factories that make up an enterprise, and between the departments that make up a factory. At times contradictions may even emerge in a work brigade, among the workers who make up the unit. A case in point would be one in which workers are paid bonuses for faster production. In such circumstances a brigade might refuse to allow one of its members to take an hour away from production to give instruction to other co-workers, since this would lower the group's productivity and thus its wages. Despite these contradictions, we are building socialism and eliminating man's exploitation by man.

D ON'T SIMILAR things occur under capitalism, in the departments of a factory that depend on one another? Could it be that the two systems have similar contradictions?

Contradictions among human beings are continually being reflected in the socialist sector. But when they are not exacerbated by deep misunderstandings or by modes of conduct that are not revolutionary, such contradictions are not antagonistic and can be resolved within the boundaries set by society.[8]

We agree that the state sector does not yet in any way constitute a single large enterprise. This stems from organizational defects, from our society's lack of development, and from the fact that two systems of financing [enterprises] exist.[9] In its fundamentals, our conception of a single enterprise is based on Marx's definition of a commodity:

> In order to become a commodity, the product must be transferred to the other person, for whom it serves as a use-value, through the medium of exchange.[10]

In a footnote Engels explains that he introduced this passage on the concept of the commodity to avoid the misconception of those who view a commodity as any product consumed by someone other than the producer. Engels noted that rents-in-kind were not commodities, since no exchange had taken place, and cited examples from feudal society.[11] Isn't it possible that this view of the commodity, with its corresponding examples, may be valid in the present, as we build socialism?

We believe that in a developed budgetary finance system, the transfer of a product from one department to another, or from one enterprise to another, cannot be viewed as an act of exchange. It is simply an act of creating or adding new value through labor.

IN OTHER WORDS, a commodity is a product that changes ownership through an act of exchange, of buying and selling. But in a budgetary finance system, in a situation where all factories are state property, such a phenomenon does not occur. The product acquires the characteristics of a commodity only when it reaches the market and passes into the hands of the consumer.

Our opinion on costs is indicated in the article mentioned earlier, appearing in this publication under my name, to which I refer the interested reader.[12]

With respect to the size of Cuba,[13] by applying Mora's criteria we could propose dividing his ministry into nine autonomous ministries, one on each floor, given its overly large size. If he doesn't see it this way, let him test it out by climbing the stairs to his office, and he'll be convinced. If instead he uses the telephone, the elevator, and the intercom, it is because they exist for this purpose. Distances in Cuba are measured by modern means of communication, not by the length of time it took our ancestors to get from one spot to another.

That covers our differences.

With our reply, a polemic is now under way. Polemics can be of considerable educational value so long as we conduct them with the greatest possible scientific rigor and objectivity. We do not shy away from confrontations. But since we are in the midst of a discussion that involves the highest levels of the government and party, where two schools of thought exist regarding the system of financing, we believe that careful attention to the form and method of the discussion is important.

We commend the initiative of Comrade Mora in entering the public arena with his criticism, although it is always better to call things by their names. We are also pleased by the quality of the magazine published by the Ministry of Foreign Trade. It sets a standard we will try to attain with our modest publication.

THE MEANING OF SOCIALIST PLANNING

A reply to Charles Bettelheim

by Ernesto Che Guevara

SSUE NO. 32 of *Cuba Socialista* [April 1964] contains an article by Comrade Charles Bettelheim entitled "Forms and Methods of Socialist Planning and the Level of Development of the Productive Forces."[1] The article takes up a number of points of considerable interest, but for us it has the added importance of being written to defend the economic accounting system and the categories that system presupposes within the socialist sector—such as money as a means of payment, credit, the commodity, and so on.

We believe two fundamental errors are committed in the article, which we will try to pinpoint.

The first error concerns the interpretation of the necessary correlation between the forces of production and the relations of production.[2] Comrade Bettelheim offers examples from the Marxist classics on this point.

During all the intermediate processes of a society's development, the productive forces and the relations of production advance together inseparably. At what point may the relations of production no longer faithfully reflect the development of the productive forces? When a society is on the ascent and advances over the previous society by shattering it; and when the old society is crumbling and the new society, whose relations of production are going to be established, is fighting to consolidate itself and to destroy the old superstructure.

At particular moments in history, therefore, the forces of

This article appeared in the June 1964 issue of Cuba Socialista. *Charles Bettelheim, a professor of economics, worked as an economic adviser in Cuba in the early years of the revolution.*

ENDNOTES FOR THIS ARTICLE BEGIN ON PAGE 201.

production and the relations of production, when analyzed concretely, are not always completely congruent. That is why Lenin could say that a socialist revolution had indeed occurred in October 1917 and then, faced with particular conditions, that it was nevertheless necessary to turn to state capitalism and to pursue a more cautious policy in relations with the peasantry. Lenin's assessment was based on his great discovery of how the world capitalist system develops.

Bettelheim says:

> . . . the decisive lever for altering human behavior lies in changes brought about in production and in the organization of production. Education essentially has the task of eradicating inherited attitudes and modes of behavior that survive from the past, and of teaching the new norms of conduct imposed by the development of the productive forces themselves.[3]

Lenin says:

> "The development of the productive forces of Russia has not attained the level that makes socialism possible." All the heroes of the Second International, including, of course, Sukhanov, beat the drums about this proposition.[4] They keep harping on this incontrovertible proposition in a thousand different keys, and think that it is the decisive criterion of our revolution.
>
> But what if the situation, which drew Russia into the imperialist world war that involved every more or less influential West-European country and made her a witness of the eve of the revolutions maturing or partly already begun in the East, gave rise to circumstances that put Russia and her development in a position which enabled us to achieve precisely that combination of a "peasant war" with the working-class movement suggested in 1856 by no less a Marxist than Marx himself as a possible prospect for Prussia?[5]
>
> What if the complete hopelessness of the situation, by stimulating the efforts of the workers and peasants tenfold, offered us the opportunity to create the fundamental requisites of civilisation in a different way from that of

the West-European countries? Has that altered the general line of development of world history? Has that altered the basic relations between the basic classes of all the countries that are being, or have been, drawn into the general course of world history?

If a definite level of culture is required for the building of socialism (although nobody can say just what that definite "level of culture" is, for it differs in every West-European country), why cannot we begin by first achieving the prerequisites for that definite level of culture in a revolutionary way, and *then,* with the aid of the workers' and peasants' government and the Soviet system, proceed to overtake the other nations?[6]

As CAPITALISM expanded into a world system, relations of exploitation developed not only between individuals within a nation but also between nations. The world capitalist system—which had become imperialism—entered into a period of shocks and conflicts, and the possibility emerged of imperialism breaking at its weakest link—tsarist Russia after World War I. From the outset of the revolution, five different types of production coexisted in Russia. As Lenin noted at the time, these were patriarchal agriculture, that is, agriculture in its most primitive form; small commodity production—including the majority of those peasants who sold their grain; private capitalism; state capitalism; and socialism.[7]

Lenin pointed out that each of these types of production existed in Russia in the period immediately after the revolution. Yet he characterized the overall system on the basis of its socialist features, even though the productive forces had not reached their full development. Obviously, when backwardness is very great, the correct Marxist course is, to the degree possible, to adjust the spirit of the new era—that is, its tendency to eliminate the exploitation of man by man—to the concrete situation of that country. That is what Lenin did in Russia recently freed from tsarism, and this was applied as a norm in the Soviet Union.

This entire approach was absolutely valid and extraordinarily perceptive at the time, and we believe it is applicable to concrete situations at particular moments in history. But those developments were followed by very important events, including the establishment of an entire world socialist system, with close to a billion inhabitants—one-third of the world's population. The continuing advance of the socialist system as a whole has influenced consciousness of peoples at all levels. That is why Cuba at a certain point in its history defined its revolution as socialist. And this affirmation of the socialist character of the revolution did not precede the establishment of the economic foundations for it—far from it.

Hᴏᴡ ᴄᴀɴ ᴀ country colonized by imperialism, with no developed basic industry, a one-crop economy, and dependent on a single market, make the transition to socialism?[8] There are a number of ways that question could be answered.

Like the theoreticians of the Second International, one can argue that Cuba has broken all the laws of dialectics, of historical materialism, and of Marxism—and thus is not a socialist country and should return to its previous situation.

On the other hand, one can be more realistic and try to find in the relations of production within Cuba the internal motor forces that brought about the revolution. But this will lead to the discovery that there are many countries in the Americas and elsewhere in the world where a socialist revolution is much more realizable than in Cuba.

There is a third explanation that, in our opinion, is the correct one. That is, in the overall framework of the world capitalist system and its struggle against socialism, one of the weak links in that system can be broken—in this case Cuba. With correct leadership from their vanguard, Cuba's revolutionary forces took advantage of special historical circumstances and conquered power. Since sufficient objective conditions already existed in Cuba in terms of the socialization of labor, they skipped stages, declared the socialist character of the revolution, and began to build socialism.

This is the dynamic, dialectical way in which we view and analyze the question of the necessary correlation between the relations of production and the development of the productive forces. The fact that the Cuban revolution took place is something that cannot escape analysis or be ignored when studying our history. And it leads us to the conclusion that since Cuba did make a socialist revolution, the conditions for a socialist revolution did therefore exist. Because to carry out a revolution without such conditions, to take power and to declare socialism by magic, is something not anticipated by any theory—and is a view I don't believe Comrade Bettelheim would support.

If socialism emerges as a concrete reality in these new conditions, it is because the development of the productive forces has come into conflict with the relations of production prior to what might rationally have been expected in a single capitalist country alone. What happens? The vanguard of the revolutionary movements, increasingly influenced by Marxist-Leninist ideology, is capable of consciously foreseeing an entire series of steps to be carried out and to force the pace of events—but to force it within the limits of what is objectively possible. We stress this point, because it is one of the main flaws in Bettelheim's argument.

Let us begin with the concrete fact that a revolution cannot be made without a fundamental contradiction between the development of the productive forces and the relations of production. Such a contradiction did exist in Cuba, and it gave the Cuban revolution socialist features. This must be acknowledged even though, upon objective analysis, an entire series of productive forces within Cuba are still in an embryonic state and not developed to the maximum. But these are the circumstances in which the revolution occurred and triumphed. So how can it be argued after the fact that there is a necessary, obligatory, rigid, and mechanical congruence between the productive forces and the relations of production? How can such an argument be used to defend, for example, the economic accounting system and to attack the system of consolidated enterprises that we have established in Cuba?[9]

To say that the consolidated enterprises are an aberration is more or less the same as saying the Cuban revolution is an aberration. The consolidated enterprises and the Cuban revolution are concepts of the same sort and flow from the same analysis. Comrade Bettelheim has never said that the Cuban socialist revolution is not an authentic one. But he does say that our present relations of production do not correspond to the development of the productive forces, and therefore he foresees big setbacks.

Comrade Bettelheim's failure to apply dialectical thought to these two concepts—distinct in magnitude, but not in tendency—is the source of his error. The consolidated enterprises emerged, developed, and continue to develop because they were able to—it is the proof of practice, as incontestable as one of Perogrullo's truisms.[10] From the most fundamental standpoint, whether one method of administration is more efficient than another is not very important, since these differences are essentially quantitative. Our system looks to the future, toward a more accelerated development of consciousness, and through consciousness, to the development of the productive forces.

Comrade Bettelheim denies that consciousness can play such a role, basing his argument on Marx's point that consciousness is a product of social circumstances, not the other way around. We will use Marx's analysis, however, to argue against Bettelheim.

Marx's assessment is absolutely correct. But in the epoch of imperialism, consciousness takes on international dimensions as well. Today's consciousness is the product of the development of the totality of productive forces throughout the world. It is also the product of the impact on the world's peoples of the teachings and education from the Soviet Union and other socialist countries.

It should be clear, therefore, that the consciousness of the vanguard in a given country, based on the general development of the productive forces, can determine the course of action necessary to lead a socialist revolution to victory in that country. This is true even if within that country—within the confines of its own borders—the contradictions between the development of the productive forces and the relations of production have not reached a level that objectively makes a revolution either essential or possible.

This brings us to Comrade Bettelheim's second serious error—his insistence on ascribing to legal or juridical structures the possibility of an independent existence. His analysis stresses the need to take relations of production into account in establishing the legal forms of ownership. To think that the legal forms of ownership—or, more accurately, the superstructure of a given state at a given time—could be imposed contrary to the realities of the relations of production is to deny the very determinism on which Comrade Bettelheim relied to express the idea that consciousness is a social product. Of course, these are historical rather than physical or chemical processes. They do not take place in thousandths of a second but rather over the long course of human existence. There are many aspects of legal relations that do not correspond to the relations of production that characterize a country at a given moment; this simply means that these aspects will be destroyed over time, as the new relations are imposed over the old. The reverse is not true, however—it is not possible to change the superstructure without first changing the relations of production.

Comrade Bettelheim repeatedly states that the nature of the relations of production is determined by the level of development of the productive forces, and that the ownership of the means of production is the legal and abstract expression of certain relations of production. He overlooks the fact that while this is perfectly true in general (whether worldwide or within a country), the microscopic correlations he attempts to establish between the exact legal relations of ownership and the level of development of the productive forces in each region or in each situation are impossible to determine.

HE ATTACKS those economists who claim to see ownership by the people of the means of production as an expression of socialism. He contends that these legal relations cannot serve as the basis of anything. In a certain sense, he may be right with regard to the word *basis*. But the essential point is that the relations of production and the development of the productive forces eventually come into conflict. And such clashes are not determined mechanically by an accumulation of economic forces. Instead, they are the sum of a quantitative and a qualitative factor: an accumulation of productive forces, considered from the point of view of economic development; and considered from the point of view of politics and history, the overthrow of one social class by another.

In other words, economic analysis cannot be separated from the historical fact of the class struggle (until we reach a perfect society). Therefore, for human beings—the living expression of the class struggle—the legal basis that represents the super-structure of the society in which they live has concrete characteristics and expresses a palpable reality. The relations of production and the development of the productive forces are economic and technological phenomena that build up over the course of history. Social ownership of the means of production is a tangible expression of these relations, just as the commodity is a concrete expression of relations between human beings. The commodity exists because there is a commodity-producing society that has given rise to a division of labor based on private ownership of the means of production. Socialism exists because there is a new kind of society in which the expropriators have been expropriated and social ownership has replaced the old, individual forms of ownership by the capitalists.

This is the general line of march the transition period should follow. Detailed relations between one or another layer of society are of interest only for certain concrete analyses. Theoretical analysis, however, should start from the overall framework of the new relations among human beings—the society in transition to socialism.

On the basis of those two fundamental conceptual errors, Comrade Bettelheim argues that at any given time and in any given place there must be an exact identity between the development of the forces of production and the relations of production. At the same time, he mixes up the relations of production with their legal expression.

What is the reason for this? Bettelheim says:

> Under these conditions, an approach that uses the general notion of "state property" to encompass the various higher forms of socialist property, seeking to reduce them to a single phenomenon, runs into insuperable difficulties. This is especially true when, on the basis of such an approach, one tries to analyze the circulation of com-

modities within the state socialist sector, socialist com-
merce, the role of money, etc.[11]

Later, analyzing the division Stalin made between two forms
of ownership,[12] Bettelheim says:

> This legal starting point [of Stalin's] and the analysis
> that stems from it lead to rejecting the present necessity
> of the commodity character of exchanges between state-
> owned socialist enterprises. On a theoretical plane, the
> nature of the buying and selling carried out between
> state enterprises, the nature of money, of prices, of eco-
> nomic accounting, of financial self-management, etc.,
> are rendered incomprehensible. These categories are
> stripped of all real social content. They appear as ab-
> stract forms or as more or less arbitrary technical proce-
> dures, not as the expression of objective economic laws
> whose necessity was noted by Stalin himself.[13]

In our view Comrade Bettelheim's article—despite its clear
opposition to ideas we have expressed on several occasions—is
undoubtedly important, since it is written by someone who is
both a very knowledgeable economist and a theoretician of
Marxism. He begins with the current situation and goes on to
make a defense—in our view, one that is not well thought
out—of the use of the categories inherent to capitalism during
the transition period, and of the need for individual ownership
within the socialist sector. In the process, he shows that a detailed analysis of the relations of production and of social ownership along Marxist lines (which we could call orthodox) is
incompatible with maintaining such categories, and says there is
something incomprehensible here.

We would say exactly the same thing, but our conclusion is
different. We believe that the inconsistency among the defenders of the economic accounting system stems from the fact that
they follow Marxist analysis to a certain point but then, in order
to continue their line of argument, have to take a leap (leaving
the "missing link" in the middle). Concretely, the defenders of
the economic accounting system have never correctly explained
how the concept of the commodity, in its essence, can be applied to transactions [among enterprises and institutions] in

the state sector. Nor have they explained how the law of value can be used "intelligently" in the socialist sector with its distorted markets.

Taking note of the inconsistency, Comrade Bettelheim restates his arguments. He begins his analysis where it should have ended—with the existing legal relations in the socialist countries and with the categories that continue to remain in existence there. Noting the obvious fact that such legal and commodity categories do indeed exist there, he concludes pragmatically that they do so because they are necessary. From this starting point, he then goes backward, in an analytical way, until he reaches the point where theory and practice collide. He then gives a new interpretation to the theory, submits Marx and Lenin to analysis, and draws his own conclusions, with the mistaken premises that we have noted. In this way, he is able to formulate a consistent process from one end of the article to the other.

He forgets, however, that the period of the transition to socialism is young historically. As human beings attain a full understanding of economic reality and begin to master it through the plan, they inevitably make errors of assessment. But why conclude that what "is" during the transition period is necessarily what "must be"? Why justify the blows dealt by reality to certain bold acts as deriving exclusively from boldness rather than—in whole or in part—from technical flaws in the way things are administered?

In our view, Bettelheim takes too much away from the importance of socialist planning—with all the technical defects it may have—when he contends:

> From this flows the impossibility of proceeding in a satisfactory way—that is, efficiently—with an overall a priori distribution of the means of production and of products in general; and the need therefore for *socialist commerce* and state commercial bodies. This is the origin of the role of money within the socialist sector itself, and of the role of the law of value. It is also the origin of the role of a system of prices that must reflect not *only* the social cost of various products but *also* their relations of supply and demand, so as to assure the possibility of balancing supply and demand when the plan has proved unable to do

so a priori, and when the use of administrative measures to do it would compromise the development of the productive forces.[14]

DESPITE OUR weaknesses (in Cuba), we nonetheless made an attempt at a fundamental definition:

> We reject the possibility of consciously using the law of value in the absence of a free market that automatically expresses the contradiction between producers and consumers. We reject the existence of the *commodity* category in relations among state enterprises. We consider all such establishments to be part of the single large enterprise that is the state (although in practice this has not yet happened in our country). The law of value and the plan are two terms linked by a contradiction and its resolution. We can therefore state that centralized planning is the essence of socialist society, its defining characteristic, and the point at which man's consciousness is finally able to synthesize and direct the economy toward its goal—the full liberation of the human being in the framework of communist society.[15]

To establish a connection between the production unit (Bettelheim's economic entity) and its degree of physical integration is to carry the mechanism to its ultimate extreme and to deny ourselves the possibility of doing what, from a technical point of view, the U.S. monopolies have already done in a number of branches of Cuban industry. It places too little confidence in our strengths and abilities.

> What may be called a "production unit" (and what constitutes a genuine economic entity) obviously varies according to the level of development of the productive forces. In certain branches of production, where the integration of operations is sufficiently advanced, the branch itself may constitute a "production unit." This may be the case, for example, in the electrical power industry, where a network of grids permits unified, centralized management of the entire branch.[16]

As we developed our system pragmatically, we were on the lookout for some of the problems discussed above. And we tried to resolve them, following as closely as possible—insofar as our education would permit—the great ideas of Marx and Lenin. This led us to seek solutions to existing contradictions in a Marxist approach to the political economy of the transition period. In trying to overcome these contradictions—which can only temporarily stand in the way of socialist development, since socialist society does in fact exist—we searched for the organizational methods best suited to practice and to theory, permitting us to advance the new society to the maximum degree through the development of consciousness and production. This is the chapter we are absorbed in now.

To CONCLUDE:

1. We believe Bettelheim commits two very big errors in his method of analysis:

(a) He takes the concept of the necessary correspondence between the relations of production and the development of the productive forces—which has overall validity—and mechanically applies it to the "microcosm" of the relations of production in concrete aspects of a single country during the transition period. He then draws conclusions that amount to apologetics—tinged with pragmatism—for the so-called economic accounting system.

(b) He applies the same mechanical analysis to the concept of ownership.

2. Therefore we do not agree with his view that financial self-management or enterprise autonomy "are linked to a given state of the productive forces." This is a conclusion that stems solely from his method of analysis.

3. We reject his concept of centralized management based on the degree of the physical centralization of production (he gives the example of an electrical power network). Instead we apply centralization to the most important economic decisions.

4. We consider his explanation of the need for unrestricted operation of the law of value and other commodity categories during the transition period to be inaccurate. At the same time,

we do not reject the possibility of using elements of this law for comparative purposes (costs, profitability in terms of money of account).

5. In our view, "centralized planning is the mode of existence of socialist society."[17] Therefore, in comparison with Bettelheim, we attribute to it a much greater power for conscious decision-making.

6. From the standpoint of theory, we believe it is extremely important to examine the inconsistencies between the classic methods of Marxist analysis and the survival of commodity categories in the socialist sector. This is an aspect that deserves more attention.

7. As for the defenders of the economic accounting system, the following, for the purposes of this article, is appropriate: "God protect me from my friends; I can protect myself from my enemies."

A Packinghouse Worker's Fight for Justice

The Mark Curtis Story

by Naomi Craine

The story of the victorious eight-year battle to defeat the political frame-up of Mark Curtis, a union activist and socialist sentenced in 1988 to twenty-five years in prison on trumped up charges of attempted rape and burglary. The pamphlet describes what happened to Curtis on the day of his arrest, the fight to defend immigrant rights he was a part of, and the international campaign that finally won his freedom in 1996. $6.00

NOTES

On the articles, books, and periodicals cited in this issue

FOR THE CONVENIENCE of our readers, we are grouping together the notes to the articles in this issue of *New International* on "Che Guevara, Cuba, and the Road to Socialism."

The full reference to a book (author, complete title, publisher, date and place of publication, and page numbers) will be listed the first time it is noted. Subsequent references will use an abbreviated reference to the book, along with the page numbers.

The initial notation of articles or speeches that first appeared in the press in Cuba will be to the original Spanish-language article and publication, together with the most easily accessible English-language translation (most often from the *Militant* newsweekly published in New York, *Granma Weekly Review* (hereinafter *GWR*) published in Havana, or a book or pamphlet published by Pathfinder Press of New York). Subsequent references to these articles will be to the English-language version.

An acquaintance with Guevara's writings will provide readers a much richer understanding of the questions under discussion in this issue. The most readily accessible of these writings by Guevara in English translation can be found in *Che Guevara and the Cuban Revolution: Writings and Speeches of Ernesto Che Guevara* (New York: Pathfinder, 1987). Readers are especially referred to part 2 on "Building Socialism in Cuba" and part 3 on "Internationalism and the Cuban Revolution."

Excerpts from Guevara's writings not otherwise available in English are quoted extensively in Carlos Tablada's book *El pensamiento económico de Ernesto Che Guevara* (The economic thought of Ernesto Che Guevara), published in English by Pathfinder as *Che Guevara: Economics and Politics in the Transition to Socialism* (New York: Pathfinder, 1990).

Below is a listing of these and other books most frequently referred to in this issue, followed by the abbreviated identification that will be used in subsequent notes.

- Ernesto Che Guevara, *Che Guevara and the Cuban Revolution: Writings and Speeches of Ernesto Che Guevara*. Hereinafter Guevara (Pathfinder).
- Ernesto Che Guevara, *Ernesto Che Guevara: Escritos y discursos* (Havana: Editorial de Ciencias Sociales, 1977). Hereinafter *Escritos*.
- Ernesto Che Guevara, *El Che en la revolución cubana* (Che in the Cuban revolution) (Havana: Ed. Ministerio del Azúcar, 1966).
- Carlos Tablada, *Che Guevara: Economics and Politics in the Transition to Socialism*. Hereinafter Tablada (Pathfinder).
- Bertram Silverman, ed., *Man and Socialism in Cuba: The Great Debate* (New York: Atheneum, 1971). Hereinafter Silverman. This book is out of print but can be found in some libraries.
- Karl Marx, *Capital*, vols. 1 and 3 (New York: Vintage, 1977 and 1981). This edition is identical to the three-volume Penguin edition published in Britain.
- Karl Marx and Frederick Engels, *Collected Works* (New York: International Publishers, 1975–). Hereinafter *MECW*.
- V.I. Lenin, *Collected Works* (Moscow: Progress Publishers, 1960-71). Hereinafter *LCW*.

Finally, two of the items frequently referred to throughout this issue are Guevara's 1965 article "Socialism and Man in Cuba" (contained in *Che Guevara and the Cuban Revolution*) and the October 8, 1987, speech by Fidel Castro, "Che's Ideas Are Absolutely Relevant Today" (contained in Tablada, *Che Guevara: Economics and Politics in the Transition to Socialism*). In addition to being available in these books, they can also be obtained in a substantially less expensive pamphlet form in Ernesto Che Guevara and Fidel Castro, *Socialism and Man in Cuba* (New York: Pathfinder, 1989).

In this issue

1. Rodríguez's article appeared in issue no. 33 (May-June 1988) of *Cuba Socialista*. In issue no. 35 the Cuban journal opened a discussion in its pages concerning the transition to socialism. Tablada's article, which appeared in issue no. 39 (May-June 1989), was a contribution to that exchange. Other articles in this debate

continued to appear through issue no. 45 (July-September 1990), after which publication of *Cuba Socialista* and numerous other Cuban periodicals and newspapers was suspended due to a severe shortage of paper and printing materials.

2. The CMEA (also sometimes called Comecon) was founded in 1949 at Moscow's initiative. Its stated purpose was to coordinate trade and investment policies of the Soviet and Eastern European workers' states. In subsequent years Mongolia (1962), Cuba (1972), and Vietnam (1978) joined the council. Yugoslavia was not a member but participated in some CMEA bodies. Albania withdrew in 1961. North Korea and China were never CMEA members or associates.

In January 1990 the CMEA announced that its trade policies would be increasingly based on world market prices, payable in hard currency. Plans to dissolve the CMEA and replace it with a looser body called the Organization for International Economic Coordination were subsequently announced.

3. Unequal exchange refers to the exploitative draining of value from the oppressed nations of the Third World not only to the imperialist countries, but also to more industrially advanced workers' states that conduct trade on the basis of world market prices. Guevara's views on this are presented in two speeches he gave at international forums in 1964 and 1965. They are "The Philosophy of Plunder Must Cease" and "At the Afro-Asian Conference," in Guevara (Pathfinder), pp. 299-320, 337-46.

4. Fidel Castro, "Che's Ideas Are Absolutely Relevant Today," in Tablada (Pathfinder), p. 45.

5. Jack Barnes, *The Changing Face of U.S. Politics: The Proletarian Party and the Trade Unions* (New York: Pathfinder, 1981).

6. *In Defense of Socialism: Four Speeches on the Thirtieth Anniversary of the Cuban Revolution* (New York: Pathfinder, 1989). *U.S. Hands Off the Mideast! Cuba Speaks Out at the United Nations* (New York: Pathfinder, 1990).

7. For further information on the rectification process in Cuba, see: "Cuba's Rectification Process: Two Speeches by Fidel Castro," including the introduction "Cuba: A Historic Moment" by Mary-Alice Waters, in *New International*, no. 6 (1987); the October 1987 speech by Fidel Castro, "Che's Ideas Are Absolutely Relevant Today," published as an introduction to Tablada's book *Che Guevara: Economics and Politics in the Transition to Socialism*, as well as the publisher's preface to that book; '*Cuba Will Never Adopt Capitalist Methods*,' by Fidel Castro (New York: Pathfinder, 1988); and Fidel Castro, *In Defense of Socialism: Four Speeches on the Thirtieth Anniversary*

of the Cuban Revolution, including the editor's introduction.

8. English translations of sixteen of the major articles from this discussion are available in Silverman.

9. An English translation of Bettelheim's article is available in Silverman, pp. 31-59.

Che's proletarian legacy
by Mary-Alice Waters

1. For an assessment of the Abrantes case, see the editorial "Saquemos las lecciones y sigamos adelante" (Let us draw the lessons and continue advancing), in *Granma,* September 2, 1989. This editorial was also printed in *GWR,* September 10, 1989, and the *Militant,* September 29, 1989. Abrantes died of a heart attack January 21, 1991, while serving his sentence.

2. In July 1989 four Cuban officials were sentenced to death for hostile acts against a foreign state, drug trafficking, and abuse of office. Those executed were Arnaldo Ochoa, a division general in the Cuban army; Antonio de la Guardia, a colonel in the Ministry of the Interior; Amado Padrón, a major in the Ministry of the Interior; and Jorge Martínez, a captain in the Cuban army. At the same trial, ten other Cuban army and Ministry of the Interior officers were convicted and sentenced to prison terms ranging from ten to thirty years.

3. In a trial July 20-21, 1989, Diocles Torralbas, a member of the Communist Party Central Committee for more than two decades, was convicted of misappropriation of resources for personal gain, embezzlement of foreign-exchange funds, and unlawful transfer of financial resources.

4. In early 1988 combined Cuban, Angolan, and Namibian forces dealt a decisive military defeat to South Africa's invading troops at Cuito Cuanavale in southern Angola. South Africa then opened negotiations leading to an accord signed in December 1988 in which Pretoria agreed to withdraw from Namibia. Describing Cuba's attitude toward the battle at Cuito Cuanavale, Fidel Castro said, "Our country staked everything by sending its best weapons and over

50,000 men." For Cuba, he said, "everything was on the line, including the revolution." Fidel Castro, speech to Council of State, July 9, 1989, in *Granma,* July 12, 1989. This speech was also printed in *GWR,* July 23, 1989, and the *Militant,* August 11, 1989.

5. The minibrigades are construction teams composed primarily of men and women who are not professional construction workers but are industrial workers, office workers, administrative personnel, teachers, and others who volunteer to be released from their regular occupations to build badly needed housing, child-care centers, schools, clinics, and other social projects. Launched at the end of 1986, the minibrigades mobilized more than thirty thousand full-time volunteers and in their first two years built more than one hundred child-care centers in Havana alone. Alongside the minibrigade movement, beginning in 1987 special large-scale volunteer construction contingents have been organized to take on major civil engineering projects such as roads and dams.

6. Raúl Castro, speech to Council of State, July 9, 1989, in *Granma,* July 11, 1989. This speech was also printed in *GWR,* July 23, 1989.

7. "Let us draw the lessons and continue advancing," in the *Militant,* September 29, 1989.

8. Fidel Castro, speech of July 9, 1989, in the *Militant,* August 11, 1989.

9. "Let us draw the lessons," in the *Militant,* September 29, 1989.

10. Robaina is paraphrasing Guevara's "Socialism and Man in Cuba." See Guevara (Pathfinder), p. 259.

11. *Granma,* July 11, 1989. Robaina's remarks were also printed in *GWR,* July 23, 1989.

12. *Granma,* July 11, 1989. Lidia Tablada's remarks were also printed in *GWR,* July 23, 1989. The quotation is from Guevara's speech to members of the Department of State Security, May 18, 1962, in *Escritos,* vol. 9, p. 220.

13. Fidel Castro, "Che's Ideas Are Absolutely Relevant Today," in Tablada (Pathfinder), p. 41.

14. Guevara, "Socialism and Man in Cuba," in Guevara (Pathfinder), pp. 253-54.

15. "Socialism and Man in Cuba," in Guevara (Pathfinder), p. 254.

16. According to Fidel Castro's October 1, 1990, speech in Pinar del Río Province marking the third anniversary of the Blas Roca

Contingent, it had expanded by that time to thirty brigades comprising more than four thousand workers.

17. Alexei Stakhanov was a coal miner publicized in the Soviet press in the 1930s for greatly surpassing production quotas. In 1935 officials of the Stalinist Soviet government initiated a movement bearing Stakhanov's name to press for similar speedup, lengthening of the workday, and piecework in other industries, with little regard for safety or quality. While substantial numbers of Soviet workers joined the movement in order to advance the progress and defense of the workers' state, the effort was marked by gross corruption and careerism among administrators and trade union functionaries (who made their respective Stakhanovs compete against one another), as well as victimization and repression against layers of workers falsely accused of economic "sabotage." For the classic assessment of Stakhanovism and its place in the degeneration of the Russian revolution, see Leon Trotsky, *The Revolution Betrayed: What Is the Soviet Union and Where Is It Going?* (New York: Pathfinder, 1972), pp. 81-84.

18. Fidel Castro, speech of October 1, 1989, in *GWR*, October 15, 1989.

19. As part of the process of returning administrative personnel to productive work, on October 5, 1990, the Communist Party of Cuba announced measures cutting by 50 percent the number of full-time party staff members.

20. Fidel Castro, "Important Problems for the Whole of Revolutionary Thought," speech given at close of deferred session of the Third Congress of the Communist Party of Cuba, December 2, 1986, in *New International*, no. 6, pp. 217, 218.

21. Guevara, "Socialism and Man in Cuba," in Guevara (Pathfinder), p. 250.

22. The basic practical and theoretical underpinnings of the budgetary finance system were outlined by Guevara in his February 1964 article "Planning and Consciousness in the Transition to Socialism ('On the Budgetary Finance System')" (hereinafter "On the Budgetary Finance System"). This article is available in Guevara (Pathfinder), pp. 203-30. A broader range of Guevara's writings on this question are cited and discussed in the volume by Tablada.

23. Fidel Castro, "Che's Ideas Are Absolutely Relevant Today," in Tablada (Pathfinder), p. 50.

24. Fidel Castro, speech of October 1, 1989, in *GWR*, October 15, 1989.

Che's contribution to the Cuban economy
by Carlos Rafael Rodríguez

1. Marcos Portal, minister of basic industry.

2. This is a reference to Carlos Tablada's book *Che Guevara: Economics and Politics in the Transition to Socialism.*

3. The economic accounting system is a method of planning and management that has been used in the Soviet Union and Eastern European countries for several decades. It relies on substantial use of capitalist market mechanisms and incentives. In the opening years of the revolutionary government in Cuba, the economic accounting system was applied in the National Institute of Agrarian Reform, headed by Carlos Rafael Rodríguez, and in the Ministry of Foreign Trade, headed by Alberto Mora; the budgetary finance system was applied in the Ministry of Industry headed by Guevara. In the mid-1970s a version of the economic accounting system was instituted throughout Cuba under the name Economic Management and Planning System, which remains in use today.

4. The New Economic Policy was adopted at the Tenth Congress of the Russian Communist Party in March 1921, following the economic devastation caused by World War I and the subsequent civil war. Aimed at reviving an economy in which industrial production had fallen to less than 20 percent of prewar levels, the measure allowed a limited return to free trade and the operation of foreign concessions alongside the nationalized sectors of the economy. For Guevara's discussion of the New Economic Policy, see "On the Budgetary Finance System," pp. 206-8. Guevara's views on the NEP are also discussed in Tablada, pp. 96-106.

5. Lenin, "The Role and Functions of the Trade Unions under the New Economic Policy," in *LCW,* vol. 33, p. 185.

6. See "The Meaning of Socialist Planning: A Reply to Charles Bettelheim," printed elsewhere in this issue.

7. To assure an equitable distribution of basic goods, rationing was introduced in Cuba in 1962. In the parallel market, which operates alongside the ration-book market, some of the same items can be purchased without rationing but at substantially higher, though still controlled, prices. Beginning in 1990, the operation of the parallel market has been subjected to increasing restrictions due to the shortages of many goods.

8. Guevara, "On the Budgetary Finance System," in Guevara (Pathfinder), p. 219.

9. "On the Budgetary Finance System," in Guevara (Pathfinder), p. 220.

10. "On the Budgetary Finance System," in Guevara (Pathfinder), p. 220.

11. Lenin, "Political Report of the Central Committee of the R.C.P.(B.), March 27, 1922," in *LCW,* vol. 33, p. 287.

12. Guevara, "Reuniones bimestrales" (Bimonthly meetings), December 21, 1963, in *El Che en la revolución cubana,* vol. 6. Cited in Tablada (Pathfinder), p. 93.

13. Guevara, "Discurso pronunciado en la Plenaria Nacional Azucarera" (Speech given at the national sugar conference), February 9, 1963, in *El Che en la revolución cubana,* vol. 4. Cited in Tablada (Pathfinder), p. 201.

14. Fidel Castro, "Informe del Comité Central del Partido Comunista de Cuba al Primer Congreso" (Report of the Central Committee of the Communist Party of Cuba to the First Congress), in *Memorias: Primer Congreso del Partido Comunista de Cuba* (Havana: Departamento de Orientación Revolucionaria del Comité Central del Partido Comunista, 1976), vol. 1, p. 76. For an English translation, see *First Congress of the Communist Party of Cuba* (Moscow: Progress Publishers, 1976).

15. Marx, "Critique of the Gotha Programme," in *MECW,* vol. 24, p. 87.

16. Guevara, "Voluntary Work Is a School for Communist Consciousness," in Guevara (Pathfinder), p. 241.

17. Guevara, "Consejos de dirección: Informe de la Empresa Consolidada de Equipos Eléctricos" (Board meetings: Report from consolidated electrical equipment enterprise), May 11, 1964, in *El Che en la revolución cubana,* vol. 6. Cited in Tablada (Pathfinder), p. 204.

18. Guevara, "Consejos de dirección," May 11, 1964, in *El Che en la revolución cubana,* vol. 6. Cited in Tablada (Pathfinder), p. 204.

19. The Economic Commission of the National Directorate of the Integrated Revolutionary Organizations (ORI—the predecessor of the Communist Party of Cuba) was established in February 1962. Osvaldo Dorticós, the third member of the commission, served as president of Cuba from July 1959 until 1976. He was a member of the Communist Party Central Committee and Political

Bureau at the time of his death in 1983.

20. Guevara's views on the transformation of labor as a central aspect of the transition to socialism are summarized in "Socialism and Man in Cuba," in Guevara (Pathfinder), pp. 253-54.

21. Marx, "Critique of the Gotha Programme," in *MECW*, vol. 24, p. 87.

22. Guevara, "Discurso pronunciado en una reunión con los directores y jefes de Capacitación de las Empresas Consolidadas y secretarios de Educación y de Trabajo de los veinticinco sindicatos nacionales de industrias" (Speech to a meeting with directors and heads of training programs of consolidated enterprises and with the secretaries of education and labor of the twenty-five national industrial unions), March 16, 1962, in *El Che en la revolución cubana*, vol. 4. Cited in Tablada (Pathfinder), p. 184.

23. Guevara, "On the Budgetary Finance System," in Guevara (Pathfinder), p. 216.

24. "On the Budgetary Finance System," in Guevara (Pathfinder), p. 213.

25. "On the Budgetary Finance System," in Guevara (Pathfinder), p. 213. Emphasis in original.

26. Guevara, "Entrevista con los delegados obreros extranjeros asistentes al acto del Primero de Mayo" (Interview with international worker delegates attending May Day celebration), May 2, 1962, in *El Che en la revolución cubana*, vol. 4. Cited in Tablada (Pathfinder), p. 193.

27. Guevara, "Comparencia en el programa de TV 'Información Pública'" (Appearance on television program "Public Information"), February 25, 1964, in *El Che en la revolución cubana*, vol. 5. Cited in Tablada (Pathfinder), pp. 203-4.

28. Guevara, "Comparencia en el programa de TV," February 25, 1964, in *El Che en la revolución cubana*, vol. 5. Cited in Tablada (Pathfinder), pp. 204-5.

29. Guevara, "Comparencia en el programa de TV," February 25, 1964, in *El Che en la revolución cubana*, vol. 5. Cited in Tablada (Pathfinder), p. 205.

30. Guevara, "Discurso pronunciado en la entrega de premios de la emulación socialista" (Speech given at ceremony presenting socialist emulation awards), in *El Che en la revolución cubana*, vol. 5. Cited in Tablada (Pathfinder), p. 206.

31. Guevara, "Consideraciones sobre los costos de producción

como base del análisis económico en las empresas sujetas al sistema presupuestario" (Considerations on the costs of production as the basis of economic analysis in enterprises organized under the budgetary finance system), June 1963, in *El Che en la revolución cubana,* vol. 1. Cited in Tablada (Pathfinder), p. 152.

32. Guevara, "The Cadres: Backbone of the Revolution," in Guevara (Pathfinder), pp. 169-70.

33. Guevara, "Comparencia en el programa de TV," February 25, 1964, in *El Che en la revolución cubana,* vol. 5. Cited in Tablada (Pathfinder), p. 211.

The creativity of Che's economic thought
by Carlos Tablada

Except where indicated, notes to this article are by Tablada. Where citations to quoted material are used, *New International* has added English-language sources where these exist.

1. Other revolutionaries and analysts prior to and at the same time as Fidel and Che had recognized this. But none of them formulated and developed the body of ideas put forward by the two Cuban leaders.

2. Fidel Castro, speech on May 1, 1966, in *Granma,* May 2, 1966. Also in *GWR,* May 8, 1966.

3. Castro, speech at the United Nations General Assembly, October 12, 1979, as chairman of the Movement of Nonaligned Countries, in *Fidel Castro Speeches: Cuba's Internationalist Foreign Policy, 1975-80* (New York: Pathfinder, 1981), p. 204. Also available in pamphlet form in *Fidel Castro at the UN: 'We Represent the Immense Majority of Humanity'* (New York: Pathfinder, 1979).

4. Guevara, "Socialism and Man in Cuba," in Guevara (Pathfinder), p. 250.

5. Guevara became head of the Industry Department of the National Institute of Agrarian Reform (INRA) October 7, 1959, and president of the National Bank seven weeks later, November 26, 1959. On February 23, 1961, the Ministry of Industry was

established with Guevara at its head.—*NI*

6. Guevara, "La clase obrera de los EE.UU.: ¿amiga o enemiga?" (The U.S. working class: friend or foe?), April 1954 (approximate date), in Ernesto Guevara Lynch, *Aquí va un soldado de América* (Here goes a soldier of the Americas) (Buenos Aires: Editorial Sudamericana/Planeta, 1987), p. 71 (hereinafter Guevara Lynch).

7. Guevara, letter from Mexico to his father, May 27, 1955, in Guevara Lynch, p. 96.

8. Guevara, letter from Mexico to his Aunt Beatriz, January 8, 1956, in Guevara Lynch, p. 122. In his letters Guevara referred to Karl Marx as St. Karl.

9. Guevara, letter from Mexico to his mother, August or September 1956 (probable date), in Guevara Lynch, pp. 148-49.

10. Guevara, letter from Mexico to Tita Infante, October 1956 (approximate date), in Guevara Lynch, p. 150.

11. Guevara, letter from Mexico to his mother, October 1956 (approximate date), in Guevara Lynch, p. 152.

12. Alfonso Bauer Paiz, interview in *Granma,* Havana, October 29, 1977. Also in Guevara Lynch, p. 157.

13. Guevara, "Reuniones bimestrales del Ministerio de Industrias en las que participaban los directores de empresas, los delegados provinciales y los viceministros" (Bimonthly meetings of the Ministry of Industry with the participation of directors of enterprises, provincial delegates, and deputy ministers), December 21, 1963, in *El Che en la revolución cubana,* vol. 6, p. 423. Cited in Tablada (Pathfinder), p. 93.

14. These are the figures given by Miguel Figueras Pérez, general director of planning and perspectives in the Ministry of Industry during the period Che headed the ministry.

15. Figure given by Figueras Pérez.

16. Raúl Castro, speech on May 1, 1968, in Camagüey, Ediciones COR, no. 8, p. 16. Also in *GWR,* May 12, 1968.

17. Guevara, "Letter to José Medero Mestre," February 26, 1964, in Guevara (Pathfinder), pp. 367-68.

18. Guevara, "On the Budgetary Finance System," in Guevara (Pathfinder), p. 220.

19. "On the Budgetary Finance System," in Guevara (Pathfinder), p. 219.

20. Guevara, "Socialism and Man in Cuba," in Guevara (Path-

finder), p. 250.

21. Guevara, "Reuniones bimestrales," December 21, 1963, in *El Che en la revolución cubana,* vol. 6, p. 423. Cited in Tablada (Pathfinder), p. 95.

22. Marx and Engels, "The German Ideology," in *MECW,* vol. 5, p. 52.

23. On July 26, 1953, Fidel Castro led an attack on the Moncada army garrison in Santiago de Cuba that marked the beginning of the revolutionary struggle against the regime of Fulgencio Batista. After the attack's failure, Batista's forces massacred more than fifty of the captured revolutionaries. Castro and others were taken prisoner, tried, and sentenced to prison. They were released in May 1955 after a public defense campaign forced Batista's regime to issue an amnesty.—*NI*

24. Guevara, *El diario del Che en Bolivia* (The diary of Che in Bolivia) (Havana: Editora Política, 1988), p. 296, entry for July 26, 1967. Also in Guevara, *The Diary of Che Guevara* (New York: Bantam Books, 1968), p. 145.

25. Guevara, "Socialism and Man in Cuba," in Guevara (Pathfinder), p. 254.

26. Guevara, "On the Budgetary Finance System," in Guevara (Pathfinder), p. 220.

27. *Accounting* is a system for developing, compiling, annotating, and presenting economic facts. As such, it enables us to establish and verify exactly how the expenditure of labor and materials matches up against production output. It provides an ideal summary of economic relations. *Cost analysis* is an instrument that makes it possible to measure with accuracy the efficiency of human productive activity. As production takes on an increasingly social character, these two instruments tend to play a greater and greater role. See Luis Alvarez Rom (finance minister in the 1960s), *Nuestra Industria, Revista Económica* (Havana), no. 1, 1963.

28. Guevara, "La planificación socialista, su significado" (The meaning of socialist planning), in *Escritos,* vol. 8, pp. 103-4. A translation of this article appears elsewhere in this issue.

29. Marx, *Capital,* vol. 1, pp. 179-80. Emphasis added.

30. (a) *First distortion*—Free-enterprise capitalism:

Cost of production (law of value) $C + V + S$

Market price $C + V + P'$

(b) *Second distortion*—Pure monopoly capitalism:

Monopoly price = price of production + monopoly factors

(c) *Third distortion*—State monopoly capitalism:

Monopoly prices along with extensive state intervention + elements of international economic relations, including such factors as:

—Transnationalization of capital and production

—Unequal exchange

—Prices set by international monopolies

—Arms race; military-industrial complex

—Policy of subsidies

—Protectionism

—Other factors

(d) *Fourth distortion*—Emergence of socialist society. Period of transition.

(e) *Total elimination*—Communist society.

31. Guevara, "Consejos de dirección: Informe de la Empresa Consolidada de Equipos Eléctricos" (Board meetings: Report from consolidated electrical equipment enterprise), May 11, 1964, in *El Che en la revolución cubana,* vol. 6, pp. 106-7. Cited in Tablada (Pathfinder), p. 204.

32. "In its general conception of how to build a communist society, the budgetary finance system is an original contribution to the theory of the transition period. But it is also more than that. It is a model of economic management and controls in the period of transition to communism. It is a model that serves as a weapon for destroying capitalist economic relations, economic categories derived from commodity production, as well as capitalist ideology. It is, in a nutshell, the driving force behind new forms of human relations and communist consciousness." Tablada (Pathfinder), p. 129.

33. See Tablada (Pathfinder), pp. 96-106. See also Guevara, "On the Budgetary Finance System" and "Socialism and Man in Cuba" in Guevara (Pathfinder), pp. 203-20, 246-61; and "The Meaning of Socialist Planning," which appears elsewhere in this issue.

34. See Fidel Castro, "Che's Ideas Are Absolutely Relevant Today," in Tablada (Pathfinder), pp. 32-57.

35. See Guevara, speech given at the United Nations Conference on Trade and Development in Geneva, Switzerland, in March 1964, and at the Second Economic Seminar of Afro-Asian Solidarity

in Algiers, Algeria, February 24, 1965. English translations are available in Guevara (Pathfinder), pp. 299-320, 337-46.

36. Guevara, "Reuniones bimestrales," October 12, 1963, in *El Che en la revolución cubana*, vol. 6, p. 387. Cited in Tablada (Pathfinder), p. 76.

37. Guevara, "Reuniones bimestrales," February 22, 1964, in *El Che en la revolución cubana*, vol. 6, p. 447.

38. Castro, "Che's Ideas Are Absolutely Relevant Today," in Tablada (Pathfinder), p. 49.

39. Guevara, "Socialism and Man in Cuba," in Guevara (Pathfinder), p. 256.

The politics of economics:
Che Guevara and Marxist continuity
by Steve Clark and Jack Barnes

1. A workers' state can be popularly referred to as socialist (as in the name Union of Soviet Socialist Republics adopted at Lenin's suggestion, or the phrase "socialist Cuba") only if two conditions obtain: (1) the domination of capitalist property relations has been broken by the toilers; and (2) a government has arisen out of such a revolution that is headed by a communist leadership—a government committed to organizing the workers and exploited farmers to reorganize economic production and distribution along lines leading toward socialism, as part of the worldwide struggle against imperialist oppression and capitalist exploitation.

The Soviet Union, the countries of Eastern Europe, and China remain workers' states, even if horribly deformed. None of them, however, can accurately be referred to as socialist in the above sense.

2. In late 1984 what was called the Central Group was formed in Cuba, composed of the president and vice presidents of the Council of Ministers, government ministers, leaders of the Communist Party Central Committee and Political Bureau, and presidents of provincial People's Power assemblies. The group was mandated to

revamp the economic plan Cuba was then working under, changing the direction of its economic priorities. In September 1988 the Central Group's functions were taken over by the Executive Committee of the Council of Ministers.

3. Fidel Castro, "Che's Ideas Are Absolutely Relevant Today," in Tablada (Pathfinder), p. 45.

4. "Che's Ideas Are Absolutely Relevant Today," in Tablada (Pathfinder), p. 50.

5. J.V. Stalin, *Economic Problems of Socialism in the U.S.S.R.* (Peking: Foreign Languages Press, 1972), p. 8.

6. Guevara, "La banca, el crédito y el socialismo" (The banking system, credit, and socialism) in *Escritos,* vol. 8, p. 48. Also in Silverman, pp. 296-316.

7. Fidel Castro, "Che's Ideas Are Absolutely Relevant Today," in Tablada (Pathfinder), p. 45.

8. "Che's Ideas Are Absolutely Relevant Today," in Tablada (Pathfinder), p. 46.

9. "Che's Ideas Are Absolutely Relevant Today," in Tablada (Pathfinder), p. 41.

10. In Guevara (Pathfinder), pp. 203-30.

11. Guevara, "On the Budgetary Finance System," in Guevara (Pathfinder), p. 218.

12. "On the Budgetary Finance System," in Guevara (Pathfinder), p. 220.

13. "On the Budgetary Finance System," in Guevara (Pathfinder), p. 219-20.

14. Engels wrote in a supplement to volume 3 of Marx's *Capital:* "To sum up, Marx's law of value applies universally, as much as any economic laws do apply, for the entire period of simple commodity production, i.e. up to the time at which this undergoes a modification by the onset of the capitalist form of production.... Thus the Marxian law of value has a universal economic validity for an era lasting from the beginning of the exchange that transforms products into commodities down to the fifteenth century of our epoch. But commodity exchange dates from a time before any written history, going back to at least 3500 B.C. in Egypt, and 4000 B.C. or maybe even 6000 B.C. in Babylon; thus the law of value prevailed for a period of some five to seven millennia." In Marx, *Capital,* vol. 3, p. 1037.

15. For the clearest explanation of this historical transition, see Marx, *Capital,* vol. 1, chapter 14, "The Division of Labour and

Manufacture," pp. 455-91, and "Machinery and Large-Scale Industry," pp. 492-639.

16. Readers will find it useful in this regard to refer to *Thomas Sankara Speaks: The Burkina Faso Revolution, 1983-87* (New York: Pathfinder, 1988). Lenin made a similar point in November 1921 about the Mongolian People's Republic in discussions with leaders of the People's Revolutionary Party of Mongolia. See Lenin, "Talk with a Delegation of the Mongolian People's Republic," in *LCW*, vol. 42, pp. 360-61.

17. In 1984 substantial aspects of commodity relations in housing were reintroduced in Cuba with the adoption by the National Assembly of legislation permitting the renting out of rooms in privately owned homes and the private sale or exchange of homes with state approval, as well as measures to encourage individual or cooperative construction efforts. This new law, consistent with the market-oriented direction of the Economic Management and Planning System, resulted in the reemergence of real estate speculation, rent gouging, and accelerated theft of building supplies, while contributing little to solving the shortage of adequate housing in Cuba. As part of rectification, a new housing law was adopted in 1988. It placed central importance on the minibrigades as a means to expand housing, rather than credits and incentives to individual family efforts and cooperatives. The private buying and selling of homes and lots was placed under closer state supervision; private rental of rooms was maintained.

18. Fidel Castro, interview in the May 25, 1987, issue of *L'Humanité*. An English translation of the interview appeared in the July 3, 1987, *Militant*.

19. Guevara, "On the Budgetary Finance System," in Guevara (Pathfinder), p. 220.

20. Lenin, "The Role and Functions of the Trade Unions under the New Economic Policy," in *LCW*, vol. 33, p. 190.

21. Guevara, "On the Budgetary Finance System," in Guevara (Pathfinder), p. 227.

22. "On the Budgetary Finance System," in Guevara (Pathfinder), p. 228.

23. "On the Budgetary Finance System," in Guevara (Pathfinder), p. 209.

24. Fidel Castro, "Che's Ideas Are Absolutely Relevant Today," in Tablada (Pathfinder), pp. 42-43.

25. Guevara, "On the Budgetary Finance System," in Guevara (Pathfinder), p. 219.

26. In the central leadership of the revolutionary government and communist movement in Cuba, Guevara above all was responsible for establishing and promoting educational and training programs and institutes for workers in order to organize them to raise their cultural level and expand their knowledge and skills.

27. Lenin wrote in February 1921: "Men's vices, it has long been known, are for the most part bound up with their virtues. This, in fact, applies to many leading Communists. For decades, we had been working for the great cause, preaching the overthrow of the bourgeoisie, teaching men to mistrust the bourgeois specialists, to expose them, deprive them of power and crush their resistance. That is a historic cause of worldwide significance. But it needs only a slight exaggeration to prove the old adage that there is only one step from the sublime to the ridiculous. Now that we have convinced Russia, now that we have wrested Russia from the exploiters and given her to the working people, now that we have crushed the exploiters, we must learn to run the country. This calls for modesty and respect for the efficient 'specialists in science and technology,' and a business-like and careful analysis of our numerous *practical* mistakes, and their gradual but steady correction. Let us have less of this intellectualist and bureaucratic complacency, and a deeper scrutiny of the practical experience being gained in the centre and in the localities, and of the available achievements of science." Lenin, "Integrated Economic Plan," in *LCW,* vol. 32, p. 145.

28. Among the many fetishes in the forms of consciousness promoted by capitalist society, those related to technology and cost accounting are among the most frequently denied, cloaked in the mantle of "scientific objectivity." Costs and accounts are approached as "things," rather than sets of arithmetic ratios that reflect certain existing social relations and distributions of wealth and income under capitalism. Technology and forms of work organization are approached as if they can, in and of themselves, promote what is called "efficiency," without regard for the fact that "efficiency" only has meaning when gauged against established goals of conflicting social classes, their forms of organization, and their historical trajectory.

Lenin, for example, has frequently been condemned by ultraleft sectarians and anarcho-syndicalists—both while he was alive and ever since—for advocating the application in factories in the young Soviet republic of some of the particular findings of the most advanced "time and motion" studies that were conducted by capitalists in order to intensify the exploitation of labor. Lenin's proposal, however, was based on the existence of a workers' state with a communist leadership that was organizing the working class to take increasing command over the control and management of state enterprises and economic and social planning in the process of advancing toward socialism, and thus had its own class goals and priorities that established prior boundaries.

In April 1918 Lenin wrote: "The Taylor system, the last word of capitalism in this respect [i.e., time-and-motion assembly line studies], like all capitalist progress, is a combination of the refined brutality of bourgeois exploitation and a number of the greatest scientific achievements in the field of analysing mechanical motions during work, the elimination of superfluous and awkward motions, the elaboration of correct methods of work, the introduction of the best system of accounting and control, etc. The Soviet republic must at all costs adopt all that is valuable in the achievements of science and technology in this field. The possibility of building socialism depends exactly upon our success in combining the Soviet power and the Soviet organisation of administration with the up-to-date achievements of capitalism. We must organise in Russia the study and teaching of the Taylor system and systematically try it out and *adapt it to our own ends*" (emphasis added). Lenin, "The Immediate Tasks of the Soviet Government," in *LCW,* vol. 27, p. 259.

29. Guevara, "A New Attitude Toward Work," in Guevara (Pathfinder), p. 168.

30. Guevara, "On the Budgetary Finance System," in Guevara (Pathfinder), p. 213.

31. "On the Budgetary Finance System," in Guevara (Pathfinder), p. 213. See also chapter 9 on "Incentive Systems" in Tablada (Pathfinder), pp. 174-201.

32. In one of the earliest statements of the foundations of a historical materialist outlook, Marx wrote in 1845 that the philosophers who espoused a mechanical "materialist doctrine that men are products of circumstance and upbringing, and that, therefore, changed men are products of other circumstances and changed upbringing, [forget] that it is men who change circumstances and that the educator must himself be educated. Hence, this doctrine is bound to divide society into two parts, one of which is superior to society. . . .

"The coincidence of the changing of circumstances and of human activity can be conceived and rationally understood only as revolutionising practice. . . .

"The philosophers," Marx said, "have only *interpreted* the world in various ways; the point, however, is to *change* it." Marx, "Theses on Feuerbach," in *MECW,* vol. 5, pp. 7-8.

33. In the same 1845 statement cited in the above footnote, Marx wrote that "the essence of man is no abstraction inherent in each single individual. In its reality it is the ensemble of the social relations." Marx, "Theses on Feuerbach," in *MECW,* vol. 5, p. 7.

34. Fidel Castro, "Che's Ideas Are Absolutely Relevant Today," in Tablada (Pathfinder), p. 44.

35. "Che's Ideas Are Absolutely Relevant Today," in Tablada (Pathfinder), p. 43.

36. Regarding the origins of the economic accounting system, Guevara wrote: "The Soviet Union, the first country to build socialism, and those that followed its example sought to create a process of planning that would be guided by broad economic results, as reflected in financial data. Relations among enterprises were left in a state of more or less free play. This was the origin of what is called economic accounting—a poor translation of a Russian term that might better be expressed as self-financing of enterprises or, more accurately, financial self-management." Guevara, "Consideraciones sobre los costos" (Considerations on costs), in *Escritos,* vol. 7, p. 98. An English translation of this article, under the title "On Production Costs and the Budgetary System," is available in Silverman, pp. 113-21.

Given Guevara's blunt honesty and integrity in dealing with the continuity of communist theory and politics, there is good reason to believe that if he viewed his proposals as built on those used in the Soviet Union during the Stalin and immediate post-Stalin period, he would have said so. Guevara closely followed experiences with various aspects of enterprise management and planning in both advanced capitalist countries and other workers' states, and he freely pointed to particular elements he considered useful. Several examples can be found in his article "Planning and Consciousness in the Transition to Socialism ('On the Budgetary Finance System')" in *Che Guevara and the Cuban Revolution,* pp. 203-30.

37. The young workers' and peasants' republic made big strides during its first years in expanding workers' control of industry and promoting the first steps toward broader administration and management by the working class. The Supreme Council of the National Economy centralized management on the basis of councils responsible for various branches of industry, comparable to the

consolidated enterprise system in Cuba. Lenin wrote in June 1918: "Communism requires and presupposes the greatest possible centralisation of large-scale production throughout the country. The all-Russia centre, therefore, should definitely be given the right of direct control over all the enterprises of the given branch of industry. The regional centres define their functions depending on local conditions of life, etc., in accordance with the general production directions and decisions of the centre. To deprive the all-Russia centre of the right of direct control over all the enterprises of the given industry throughout the country . . . would be regional anarcho-syndicalism, and not communism." Lenin, "Comments on the Draft 'Regulations for the Management of the Nationalised Enterprises,'" in *LCW*, vol. 42, p. 96.

38. One of the major factors that gave impetus to the launching of the rectification process in 1986 was the conviction by central leaders of the Communist Party that the consequences of the reliance on economic and political methods borrowed from the Soviet and Eastern European workers' states was promoting political and moral degeneration within the party itself. The party "was starting to go to pot," Fidel Castro warned in his speech on the rectification process to the Deferred Session of the Third Congress of the Communist Party of Cuba in December 1986. See "Important Problems for the Whole of International Revolutionary Thought," by Fidel Castro, in *New International*, no. 6, p. 217.

39. Guevara, "Reuniones bimestrales" (Bimonthly meetings), December 21, 1963, in *El Che en la revolución cubana*, vol. 6, p. 425. Cited in Fernando Martínez, *Che: El socialismo y el comunismo* (Havana: Casa de las Américas, 1989) p. 134. Pointing to the importance of making these and other writings by Guevara more readily available, Martínez writes elsewhere in the book that the bibliography to Carlos Tablada's book *Che Guevara: Economics and Politics in the Transition to Socialism*, published by Pathfinder, "lists the complete contents of six of the seven volumes of *El Che en la revolución cubana* . . . thereby permitting the reader to be aware of at least the titles of a large number of these texts. I am confident that one of the results of the impulse given by Fidel to the study of Che's ideas since 1987 will be that this rare, carefully guarded edition, of which only a tiny number of copies were printed, will be republished as part of the indispensable and unpostponable publication of Che's works." Martínez, p. 35.

40. Lenin, "Ninth All-Russia Congress of Soviets: Report of the All-Russia Central Executive Committee and the Council of

People's Commissars, December 23, 1921," in *LCW,* vol. 33, pp. 158, 160.

41. We use the term *interchange* rather than *exchange* since we are speaking of the circulation and distribution of the products of social labor under socialism, which will be organized on the basis of human needs, not exchange-values determined through the market. In the evolution of human society, the "exchange" of commodities (that is, products of social labor produced not for the direct use of the producers but in order to be exchanged either for other commodities—barter—or later in history for money) arose in tandem with the emergence of class divisions and the first forms of private rather than communal property, the family, and the state. For a discussion of the evolution from the socially organized interchange of the products of social labor in the earliest forms of human society to commodity exchange in class-divided society, see Evelyn Reed, *Woman's Evolution* (New York: Pathfinder, 1975): "The Interchange System," pp. 211-71, and "The Origin of Private Property," pp. 412-15; and *Sexism and Science* (New York: Pathfinder, 1978): "The Misconceptions of Lévi-Strauss," pp. 148-49, 155-57.

42. Lenin, "Eleventh Congress of the R.C.P.(B.): Political Report of the Central Committee, March 27, 1922," in *LCW,* vol. 33, p. 287.

43. Lenin, "Eleventh Congress of the R.C.P.(B.): Speech in Opening the Congress, March 27, 1922," in *LCW,* vol. 33, p. 279.

44. Lenin, *LCW,* vol. 33, p. 280.

45. Lenin, "Speech at a Plenary Session of the Moscow Soviet, November 20, 1922," in *LCW,* vol. 33, p. 442.

46. Lenin, "On Co-operation," in *LCW,* vol. 33, p. 468.

47. *LCW,* vol. 30, p. 109.

48. Lenin's writings on these questions from the last year of his politically active life can be found in volume 33 of his *Collected Works.* Following Lenin's final debilitating stroke in early 1923, a section of the Bolshevik leadership led by Joseph Stalin and Nikolai Bukharin sought—among other rationalizations for their adaptation to the petty-bourgeois class interests of the expanding privileged bureaucratic layers and petty exploiters—to present the NEP as a strategic course toward socialism rather than a tactical retreat. The record of the political fight by others in the Bolshevik leadership to maintain Lenin's communist perspectives against this rightist trajectory is contained in the three-volume Pathfinder collection *The Challenge of the Left Opposition.* This collection contains documents of the Marxist resistance to Stalin and Bukharin's course in

the 1920s that was led by Leon Trotsky, as well as for various periods of time by E.V. Preobrazhensky, Karl Radek, Christian Rakovsky, and others.

49. Guevara, "On the Budgetary Finance System," in Guevara (Pathfinder), pp. 207-8.

50. Guevara, "Socialism and Man in Cuba," in Guevara (Pathfinder), p. 259.

51. See "Land Reform and Farm Cooperatives in Cuba," in *New International,* no. 4. This feature includes two speeches by Fidel Castro, a resolution of the Communist Party of Cuba, and an introduction by Mary-Alice Waters. Cuba's experience with land reform and the worker-peasant alliance is also discussed in two other articles in the same issue of *New International:* "The Crisis Facing Working Farmers," by Doug Jenness, and "The Fight for a Workers' and Farmers' Government in the United States," by Jack Barnes.

52. Castro announced the decision to close the farmers' market in a May 18, 1986, speech to the Second National Meeting of Agricultural Production Cooperatives held in Havana. The speech can be found in English translation in the June 1, 1986, issue of *GWR* and in the July 14, 1986, issue of *Intercontinental Press* magazine.

53. Guevara, "On the Budgetary Finance System," in Guevara (Pathfinder), p. 220.

54. Engels, "The Communists and Karl Heinzen," in *MECW,* vol. 6, pp. 303-4. A few months later, this understanding, jointly arrived at by Engels and Karl Marx in the mid-1840s, was incorporated at the heart of the founding program of the modern communist workers' movement drafted by Marx and Engels for the conference launching the international Communist League in December 1847. That document, the Manifesto of the Communist Party (commonly referred to as the Communist Manifesto), explained:

"The theoretical conclusions of the Communists are in no way based on ideas or principles that have been invented, or discovered, by this or that would-be universal reformer. They merely express, in general terms, actual relations springing from an existing class struggle, from a historical movement going on under our very eyes."

Communists, the Manifesto said, "have no interests separate and apart from those of the proletariat as a whole. They do not set up any sectarian principles of their own, by which to shape and mould the proletarian movement."

The only things that distinguish communists in the working class from others they work and fight alongside, Marx and Engels explained, are: "1. In the national struggles of the proletarians of the different countries, [communists] point out and bring to the front the common interests of the entire proletariat, independently of all nationality. 2. In the various stages of development which the struggle of the working class against the bourgeoisie has to pass through, they always represent the interests of the movement as a whole.

"The Communists, therefore, are on the one hand, practically, the most advanced and resolute section of the working-class parties of every country, that section which pushes forward all others; on the other hand, theoretically, they have over the great mass of the proletariat the advantage of clearly understanding the line of march, the conditions, and the ultimate general results of the proletarian movement." Marx and Engels, "Manifesto of the Communist Party," in *MECW*, vol. 6, pp. 496-97.

55. Guevara, "On the Budgetary Finance System," in Guevara (Pathfinder), p. 224.

56. More accurate assessments and statistics released by official Soviet government institutions themselves in recent years indicate that both the absolute size of the output of Soviet industry and its breadth of technological development have been previously overestimated by friend and foe alike.

On the concept of value
by Ernesto Che Guevara

1. Alberto Mora fought in the Cuban revolution as a leader of the Revolutionary Directorate and was imprisoned by the Batista dictatorship. One of the youngest ministers in the new revolutionary government, he served as director of the Bank for Foreign Trade and later, until 1964, as minster of foreign trade.

2. An English translation of the article is available in Silverman.

3. Marx, *Capital*, vol. 1, p. 129.

4. Guevara, "Consideraciones sobre los costos" (Considerations on costs), in *Escritos*, vol. 7, p. 98. An English translation of this

article is available under the title "On Production Costs and the Budgetary System," in Silverman, pp. 113-21.

5. Lenin noted that at times of great unrest imperialism might break first at its "weakest link." In his speech marking the first anniversary of the October revolution, he said: "We have always realised that it was not on account of any merit of the Russian proletariat, or because it was in advance of the others, that we happened to begin the revolution, which grew out of world-wide struggle. On the contrary, it was only because of the peculiar weakness and backwardness of capitalism, and the peculiar pressure of military strategic circumstances, that we happened in the course of events to move ahead of the other detachments, while not waiting until they had caught us up and rebelled." Lenin, "Extraordinary Sixth All-Russia Congress of Soviets: Speech on the Anniversary of the Revolution, November 6, 1918," in *LCW,* vol. 28, pp. 137-38.

6. In a postscript to the first edition of *The State and Revolution,* dated November 30, 1917, Lenin explains: "I was 'interrupted' by a political crisis—the eve of the October revolution of 1917. Such an 'interruption' can only be welcomed; but the writing of the second part of the pamphlet . . . will probably have to be put off for a long time. It is more pleasant and useful to go through the experience of the revolution than to write about it." Lenin, *LCW,* vol. 25, p. 497.

7. *Effective demand,* as contrasted to *demand,* denotes that portion of social needs that can actually be met given society's corresponding money and resources.

8. *Nonantagonistic contradictions* is a term used to denote differences that are not based on the conflicting interests of hostile social classes.

9. The two systems of financing referred to are the *budgetary finance system,* developed by Guevara and implemented at the time in enterprises under the direction of the Ministry of Industry; and the *economic accounting system,* implemented in the remainder of the Cuban economy.

10. Marx, *Capital,* vol. 1, p. 131.

11. The passage from Marx's *Capital* cited by Guevara and footnoted by Engels is as follows: "A thing can be useful, and a product of human labour, without being a commodity. He who satisfies his own need with the product of his own labour admittedly creates use-values, but not commodities. In order to produce the latter, he must not only produce use-values, but use-values for others, social

use-values. (And not merely for others. The medieval peasant produced a corn-rent for the feudal lord and a corn-tithe for the priest; but neither the corn-rent nor the corn-tithe"—what Guevara in this article calls "rents-in-kind"—"became commodities simply by being produced for others. In order to become a commodity, the product must be transferred to the other person, for whom it serves as a use-value, through the medium of exchange.)"

In his footnote to this passage in the fourth German edition of *Capital* (1890), Engels states: "I have inserted the passage in parentheses because, through its omission, the misconception has very frequently arisen that Marx regarded every product consumed by someone other than the producer as a commodity." In Marx, *Capital*, vol. 1, p. 131.

12. Guevara, "Consideraciones sobre los costos," in *Escritos*, vol. 7, pp. 97-107.

13. In the article that Guevara is responding to, Mora stated: "It should be pointed out that Cuba, despite being a relatively small country, is not really so small (just try to cross Cuba on foot). The Cuban economy presents plenty of complexities." Alberto Mora, "On the Operation of the Law of Value in the Cuban Economy," in Silverman, pp. 227-28.

The meaning of socialist planning
by Ernesto Che Guevara

1. The article by Charles Bettelheim, "Formas y métodos de la planificación socialista y nivel de desarrollo de las fuerzas productivas" (Forms and methods of socialist planning and the level of development of productive forces), can also be found in Guevara, *El socialismo y el hombre nuevo* (Socialism and the new man) (Mexico City: Siglo Veintiuno, 1979), pp. 330-53. An English translation of the article, under the title "On Socialist Planning and the Level of Development of the Productive Forces," is available in Silverman, pp. 31-59.

2. Marx summarized the interrelationship between forces of production and means of production as follows: "In the social production of their existence, men inevitably enter into definite

relations, which are independent of their will, namely relations of production appropriate to a given stage in the development of their material forces of production. The totality of these relations of production constitutes the economic structure of society, the real foundation, on which arises a legal and political superstructure and to which corresponds definite forms of social consciousness. The mode of production of material life conditions the general process of social, political and intellectual life. It is not the consciousness of men that determines their existence, but their social existence that determines their consciousness.

"At a certain stage of development, the material productive forces of society come into conflict with the existing relations of production or—this merely expresses the same thing in legal terms—with the property relations within the framework of which they have operated hitherto. From forms of development of the productive forces these relations turn into their fetters. Then begins an era of social revolution. The changes in the economic foundation lead sooner or later to the transformation of the whole immense superstructure.

"In studying such transformations it is always necessary to distinguish between the material transformation of the economic conditions of production, which can be determined with the precision of natural science, and the legal, political, religious, artistic, or philosophic—in short, ideological forms in which men become conscious of this conflict and fight it out. Just as one does not judge an individual by what he thinks about himself, so one cannot judge such a period of transformation by its consciousness, but, on the contrary, this consciousness must be explained from the contradictions of material life, from the conflict existing between the social forces of production and the relations of production.

"No social order is ever destroyed before all the productive forces for which it is sufficient have been developed, and new superior relations of production never replace older ones before the material conditions for their existence have matured within the framework of the old society. Mankind thus inevitably sets itself only such tasks as it is able to solve, since closer examination will always show that the problem itself arises only when the material conditions for its solution are already present or at least in the course of formation." Marx, *A Contribution to the Critique of Political Economy* (New York: International Publishers, 1970), pp. 20-21.

3. Bettelheim, "On Socialist Planning," in Silverman, p. 33.

4. "Heroes of the Second International" refers to Karl Kautsky and other socialists who supported the bourgeois governments of

their respective countries during World War I and opposed the October revolution under the ideological cover that conditions in Russia were ripe only for a bourgeois-democratic revolution, not a socialist one. Among this current were the Mensheviks, a grouping that originated as a minority faction of the Russian Social Democratic Labor Party at its second congress in 1903, in opposition to the majority (Bolsheviks) of the party led by Lenin. The Mensheviks not only opposed the workers and peasants taking power but participated in the procapitalist Provisional Government following the February 1917 revolution and became active in counterrevolutionary activity to bring down the Soviet republic established by the October 1917 revolution. In this 1923 article Lenin is replying to N.N. Sukhanov, a member of the Mensheviks from 1909 to 1919, who wrote the seven-volume *Notes on the Revolution.*

5. Assessing the prospects for a revolutionary upsurge in Germany, Marx wrote the following in an 1856 letter to Engels: "The whole thing in Germany will depend on the possibility of backing the proletarian revolution by some second edition of the Peasant War. Then the affair will be splendid." Marx, letter to Engels of April 16, 1856, in *Selected Correspondence* (Moscow: Progress Publishers, 1975), p. 86. The text of the letter in another translation is also found in *MECW,* vol. 40, pp. 37-41.

6. Lenin, "Our Revolution," in *LCW,* vol. 33, pp. 478-79.

7. Lenin, "Left-Wing Childishness and the Petty-Bourgeois Mentality," in *LCW,* vol. 27, pp. 335-36.

8. The crop Guevara is referring to is sugar, which in 1959 accounted for about 80 percent of Cuba's exports and more than 70 percent of the country's arable land. The single market is the United States.

9. Under Guevara's leadership, the Ministry of Industry sought to merge the planning and administration of production units in the same industry throughout Cuba into a single consolidated enterprise. The Consolidated Petroleum Enterprise, for example, was created by the merger of three imperialist-owned refineries that were expropriated (Esso, Texaco, and Shell).

10. Perogrullo is a fictional character noted for stating the obvious. In *Don Quixote,* Sancho Panza describes Perogrullo as someone who would tell you "a closed hand is a fist."

11. Bettelheim, "On Socialist Planning," in Silverman, p. 48.

12. In the pamphlet *Economic Problems of Socialism in the U.S.S.R.,* Stalin described the continuing role of commodity exchanges in

the Soviet Union by making a distinction between (1) enterprises in which "the means of production and the product of production are national property," and (2) collective farms that are not state owned and—unlike state enterprises—"will not recognize any other economic relation with the town except the commodity relation—exchange through purchase and sale." Stalin, *Economic Problems of Socialism in the U.S.S.R.*, p. 15.

13. Bettelheim, "On Socialist Planning," in Silverman, p. 49.

14. Bettelheim, "On Socialist Planning," in Silverman, p. 52.

15. Guevara, "On the Budgetary Finance System," in Guevara (Pathfinder), p. 220.

16. Bettelheim, "On Socialist Planning," in Silverman, p. 44.

17. Guevara, "On the Budgetary Finance System," in Guevara (Pathfinder), p. 220.

Nueva Internacional

UNA REVISTA DE POLITICA Y TEORIA MARXISTAS

Número 4. **La marcha del imperialismo hacia el fascismo y la guerra** $15.00

Número 3. **El ascenso y el ocaso de la revolución nicaragüense** $15.00

Número 2. **Che Guevara, Cuba y el camino al socialismo**
Artículos por Ernesto Che Guevara, Carlos Rafael Rodríguez, Carlos Tablada, Mary-Alice Waters, Steve Clark y Jack Barnes $12.00

Número 1. **Los cañonazos iniciales de la tercera guerra mundial** por Jack Barnes $13.00

Nouvelle Internationale

UNE REVUE DE POLITIQUE ET DE THÉORIE MARXISTES

N° 5. **La marche de l'imperialisme vers le fascisme et la guerre** $15.00

N° 4. **Les premières salves de la troisième guerre mondiale** par Jack Barnes $13.00

N° 3. **Le deuxième assassinat de Maurice Bishop** par Steve Clark $11.00

N° 2. **La révolution à venir en Afrique du Sud** par Jack Barnes $11.00

N° 1. **Le communisme et la lutte pour un gouvernement révolutionnnaire populaire** articles de Mary-Alice Waters et Joseph Hansen.· **Leur Trotsky et le nôtre** par Jack Barnes $11.00

Ny International

TIDSKRIFT FÖR MARXISTISK POLITICK OCH TEORI

No. 2. **Imperialismens marsch mot fascism och krig** $19.00

No. 1. **De första skotten i tredje världskriget** av Jack Barnes · **Kommunistisk politik i krig och fred** av Mary-Alice Waters $19.00

New International

A MAGAZINE OF MARXIST POLITICS AND THEORY

New International no. 10

Imperialism's March toward Fascism and War *by Jack Barnes* • What the 1987 Stock Market Crash Foretold • Defending Cuba, Defending Cuba's Socialist Revolution *by Mary-Alice Waters* • The Curve of Capitalist Development *by Leon Trotsky* $14.00

New International no. 9

The Triumph of the Nicaraguan Revolution • Washington's Contra War and the Challenge of Forging Proletarian Leadership • The Political Degeneration of the FSLN and the Demise of the Workers and Farmers Government $14.00

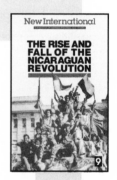

New International no. 8

The Politics of Economics: Che Guevara and Marxist Continuity *by Steve Clark and Jack Barnes* • Che's Contribution to the Cuban Economy *by Carlos Rafael Rodríguez* • On the Concept of Value *and* The Meaning of Socialist Planning *two articles by Ernesto Che Guevara* $10.00

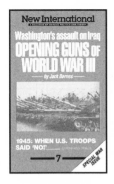

New International no. 7

Opening Guns of World War III: Washington's Assault on Iraq *by Jack Barnes* • Communist Policy in Wartime as well as in Peacetime *by Mary-Alice Waters* • Lessons from the Iran-Iraq War *by Samad Sharif* $12.00

New International no. 6

The Second Assassination of Maurice Bishop *by Steve Clark* • Washington's 50-year Domestic Contra Operation *by Larry Seigle* • Land, Labor, and the Canadian Revolution *by Michel Dugré* • Renewal or Death: Cuba's Rectification Process *two speeches by Fidel Castro* $10.00

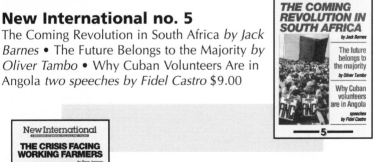

New International no. 5

The Coming Revolution in South Africa *by Jack Barnes* • The Future Belongs to the Majority *by Oliver Tambo* • Why Cuban Volunteers Are in Angola *two speeches by Fidel Castro* $9.00

New International no. 4

The Fight for a Workers and Farmers Government in the United States *by Jack Barnes* • The Crisis Facing Working Farmers *by Doug Jenness* • Land Reform and Farm Cooperatives in Cuba *two speeches by Fidel Castro* $9.00

New International no. 3

Communism and the Fight for a Popular Revolutionary Government: 1848 to Today *by Mary-Alice Waters* • 'A Nose for Power': Preparing the Nicaraguan Revolution *by Tomás Borge* • National Liberation and Socialism in the Americas *by Manuel Piñeiro* $8.00

New International no. 2

The Aristocracy of Labor: Development of the Marxist Position *by Steve Clark* • The Working-Class Fight for Peace *by Brian Grogan* • The Social Roots of Opportunism *by Gregory Zinoviev* $8.00

New International no. 1

Their Trotsky and Ours: Communist Continuity Today *by Jack Barnes* • Lenin and the Colonial Question *by Carlos Rafael Rodríguez* • The 1916 Easter Rebellion in Ireland: Two Views *by V.I. Lenin and Leon Trotsky* $8.00